A Hayes River Odyssey

John Kudlas

Copyright © 2022 John Kudlas
All rights reserved
First Edition

Fulton Books
Meadville, PA

Published by Fulton Books 2022

ISBN 978-1-63985-541-4 (paperback)
ISBN 978-1-63985-542-1 (digital)

Printed in the United States of America

Dedication

To my wife, Donna, who patiently waited and prayed for me while on my odyssey and my many other adventures.

Contents

Acknowledgments 7
Introduction 9
      Member Voyagers 11
1   The Celebration 17
2   In the Beginning 27
3   The Shakedown Cruise 35
4   Final Preparations 39
5   Henry Hudson and His Travels 43
6   The Hayes River 45
7   To Canada 50
      Departure 50
      Canada Travel Requirements 51
      Wabowden 52
      Itinerary 54
8   Delight of Flight 55
9   Daily Journal 59
      First Water 60
      The Long Portage 65
      Sailing the Hayes 67
      Windy Lake Hordes 71
      Oxford Lake Monster 74
      Marooned on Oxford Lake 76
      A Day of Toil, Disappointment, and Joy 79
      Whitewater Problems and Piscatorial Prizes 83
      More Sailing and Island Respite 85
      Sweet Day That Turned Sour 88
      A Day of Anticipation 90

	French Cuisine	91
	Successful Rapids Running	93
	Moose Encounter!	96
	Boring Water	98
	Gods River at Last	101
	Torture Aboard the Ship	102
	Hudson Bay at Last	103
	Arriving at the bay	105
	York Factory Sojourn	111
	Marooned at York Factory	119
	Decision Time	120
	Change in Plans	123
	Riding the Rails	128
	Home at Last	132
10	The Daily Routine	134
11	Running the Rapids	141
12	Sailing	149
	Building the Sailing Boat	163
13	The Hudson Bay Sojourn	167
14	Artifacts	172
15	The Cemetery	174
16	Northern Lights	177
17	Fishing	179
	Fishing Rules	188
18	Doug McLachlan	190
19	Oh, Canada!	198
20	The Nature of Adventure	200

Afterword 205
The Price of Time 207
Appendix 209

Acknowledgments

I would like to thank a number of individuals and organizations that helped us plan and complete *A Hayes River Odyssey*. First and foremost, I would like to thank my fellow accompanying voyagers that were instrumental in planning and completing the voyage. They were hardworking, learned, competent, and especially patient with me. Steve Linquist provided most of the pictures that included me (there were no selfies at the time). As I now sit at my desk in Homosassa, Florida, reliving our voyage, I miss them! Needless to say, I would also like to thank all our wives and loved ones who waited and wondered for the weeks we were gone. How great it was to receive their embraces when we returned.

    I would also like to thank the Manitoba Department of Natural Resources, Parks Branch, for the wonderful historical maps and other information they provided upon request. They were very cordial, prompt, and helpful. The Royal Canadian Mounties should also be thanked for all their helpful advice and concern for our well-being and safety. Especially important are the volunteers who maintain York Factory and the York Factory historian, Doug MacClachlan, who filled us with information. I would also like to thank and credit Wikipedia for information about Canada, our airplanes, the Hayes River, and York Factory.

Introduction

Let me then die ingloriously and without struggle, but let me first do some great thing that shall be told among men hereafter.
—Homer (*Iliad*)

Life is but an odyssey.

And anxious rivers like the Hayes are metaphoric venues for adventuresome people engaged in an odyssey of discovery. These rivers and rapids are like life experiences that we float through and sometimes struggle with. They contain "flat" water that might appear to be boring and benign and yet periodically contain rapids to test and challenge us. These rapids, like life experiences, come in various categories. First, there are expectant rapids that are vocal and alarming that we prepare for. And yet there are rapids that sneak up on us by starting with small riffle warnings and amplify into crashing, potentially life-changing catastrophes. These are the most challenging and sometimes traumatizing yet enlightening. They are run through successfully by our training, experiences, and common sense. The value of each rapids and life experience is the knowledge and the grit they render, not necessarily the end goal achieved. To develop knowledge and grit requires endurance, patience, and respect for the challenge. Joy of discovery should be an end result of the challenging odyssey. Rivers and life.

Odysseus, the hero in Homer's *Odyssey*, described his twenty years traveling home from the Trojan War in this epic poem. He graphically described his many learning experiences about the world and himself. It was a long, arduous journey in quest for a noble goal, and this journey also became a spiritual and psychological one.

Merriam-Webster describes an odyssey as "a long journey full of adventures; a series of experiences that give knowledge or understanding to someone or a voyage usually marked by many changes of fortune; an intellectual or spiritual wandering or quest." So it was for our team of voyagers.

First, I apologize to my fellow voyagers! *A Hayes River Odyssey* took place during the summer of 1983 after several months of planning. I kept copious notes of our meetings and carefully documented the voyage via a daily journal. I began writing this text shortly after the voyage and roughed out much of it during the '90s. After retiring and moving to Northern Wisconsin, all the materials lay dormant in my files as I became involved in other projects on the lakes, at schools, and at the Cable Natural History Museum. Now that I am fully retired in Florida, I am trying to catch up on my writing projects. Foremost is documenting the Hayes River odyssey!

I also apologize for the language and tone of some of the dialogue. I tried to write this as written in my rough journal for accuracy and authenticity, and I apologize to anyone who might be offended by aged language usage.

Also, be advised that this was an odyssey that was unsupported by any commercial group and that we safely completed the trek without exotic equipment or outside assistance. There is a certain joy in accomplishing tasks "the hard way" on a shoestring. Remember, this was before cell phones and the GPS. Once we left, communication with the rest of the world, especially our families, was difficult. And all our navigation was by dead reckoning with compass and topo maps. We had no idea of what was happening in the world or what the weather forecasts were. We wanted to plan and complete the expedition ourselves without aid or outside support. We had a wonderful, dynamic crew working together like a well-oiled machine in joyful toil. Please join us! I hope you enjoy our odyssey!

Member Voyagers

Author John Kudlas cranking the paddle in the rapids

John Kudlas, PhD, was a biology and ecology instructor at Mayo High School in Rochester, Minnesota. He retired to Barnes, Wisconsin, to work as a lake aquatic plant coordinator, a codeveloper of Lake Ecology Education Program (LEEP) for the Drummond School, and a taxidermist—collections monitor at Cable Natural History Museum. He presently retired to Homosassa, Florida, where he volunteers at Ellie Schiller Homosassa Springs Wildlife State Park and, of course, kayaks the many manatee rivers and fishes in the gulf.

Lee Riegler preparing "cheesecake" aboard the ship

    Lee Riegler was a youth leader at Rochester Covenant Church. He moved to the youth patient care at Mayo Clinic and later to another leadership role at the clinic. Lee and his wife, Marylyn, along with Lee's parents built a cabin next to us in Northern Wisconsin. Lee was our treasurer and land leader, keeping track of all finances and overland routes.

Master chef Mike Heinle preparing dinner

Mike Heinle, MD, was a fellow at the Mayo Clinic and was one of our medics and our head chef. The last I heard from Mike was that he was in Alaska. I contacted him before going caribou hunting but was unable to connect with him. I heard he had MS, and a fellow doctor reported that he unfortunately passed away many years ago and stated that "he was a great physician and mentor."

Bill Law, waterproofing equipment

Bill Law Jr., MD, was also a fellow at the Mayo Clinic and was also one of our medics. He and Mike put together the important first aid kit and taught us basic first aid. The last I heard about Bill was that he was in medical practice in Tennessee.

Dennis Levicky preparing breakfast aboard the ship

Dennis Levicky was an airplane mechanic at the airport in Rochester and an excellent mechanic. He loved rock climbing and riding his Harley. Last I heard, he was retired in Arizona.

Steve Linquist and I waiting in the eddies for the
next canoe to pass through the rapids

Steve Linquist was a wonderful outdoorsman and loved canoeing and climbing. He was involved in various occupations, but the last I heard, he was involved with cell phone and radio antenna work. Heights did not bother him. He was a free spirit and often slept in his beat-up white van we called the "pile of yellow snow."

The genesis of the expedition was hearing from a team that had completed the trip and reading *Canoeing with the Cree* (published in 1935) by Eric Sevareid. Eric, age seventeen, and Walter C. Port, age nineteen, canoed all the way from the Twin Cities to Hudson Bay via the Red River of the North, Lake Winnipeg, and Gods River in 1930. They covered 2,250 miles and required sixty portages, and the trip lasted nearly four months.

We learned several groups canoe the Hayes River every year and decided to communicate with a group that had recently run the Hayes. We all had tight schedules, so we knew our expedition would have to be delineated to one river—the Hayes.

So sit back, grab your paddle, and join us on the Hayes River odyssey!

Chapter 1

The Celebration

Celebrations infuse life with passion and purpose.
They summon the human spirit.
—Terrence E. Deal

We were home, safe, and dry, and the voyage odyssey was over. The completion of any adventuresome endeavor mandates a celebration, and we were ready.

I just sat in the noisy, music-infested pizza parlor and studied each of the voyagers who accompanied me on the Hayes River in Manitoba, Canada. I remembered specific things about each man, some serious and some humorous, but all carried good and warm feelings of how we cared for each other while cascading down this historic river. Like each section of the river, each man was now special.

I glanced over at Mike Heinle, who was sitting with his wife, Margarette Oakes, and remembered all those wonderful meals he had prepared while we were on the river. It was odd not seeing him kneeling in joyful toil in front of vibrating pots. Like a xylophone player, he moved to the fire's unwritten music with his baton-like cooking spoon, orchestrating gastric delights. Oh, how we enjoyed watching the maestro work, preparing food with a French chef's pride to satisfy five smelly companions.

Mike was a good-sized man is his forties. He stood tall and weighed about 210 pounds. He wore a long floppy mustache that he continually twisted and curled in a vain attempt to train it to stick straight out like handlebars. He wore glasses that he would continually push back on his nose when he was not working on his mustache. He guarded his glasses because he was nearly blind without them. He walked with a slight shuffle and slightly stooped over from dodging obstacles most short people do not notice. He always looked down at his feet while he walked and shuffled his feet (while twisting his mustache and pushing his glasses); it was almost like he was trying to learn to tap dance. He was intelligent and very learned. He would always have something to read, and his comprehension was great. He knew a great deal about any subject and could usually recite his source of information. Information gathering was important to him. His prolific reading and comprehension skills kept our trivial questions answered.

Mike was also a compassionate person. He always concerned himself with the group's health and our attitude. He always sought advice first and ate last—quite a gentleman in bush country. However, he was almost as uncoordinated as he was compassionate. He was always dropping and losing something. I felt bad when he prepared a special dinner dish then stumbled and spilled it over the guilty rocks. He also dropped his honing rod overboard before I could borrow it, and he lost the tip section of his spinning rod before he had a chance to catch a fish. His eyesight limited his coordination a great deal, but it did not limit his compassion.

Mike left for Alaska the next summer to be a staff doctor at a remote Indian village clinic. Having completed his residency at the Mayo Clinic, he was prepared to serve in the medical world. He was more interested in serving than affluence. Undoubtedly, he could make a great deal of money with his knowledge and skills, but he was not interested in material wealth. When I queried him, he simply stated, "I'm not interested in a Mercedes-Benz."

I am proud to have known Mike; we need more people like him. But most of all, I will never forget his cooking and his meticulous care and consideration of detail. Whenever I hear popple wood snapping in the fire, I will think of Mike in front of the fire, tending the coals.

Next, I turned my attention to Dennis Levicky and his wife, Betty, and remembered his many yarns. He was the oldest member of the group and was at the life stage where his many experiences were manufactured into narrations. There were mountain-climbing stories, Air Force stories, and boyhood stories of life on the Minnesota farm. He kept Steve in awe as he listened with magnetic interest. Denny would always giggle and drop his head at the conclusion of each tale. The stories were often so good that I began questioning their validity. Then I realized it did not really matter. The entertainment kept our spirits up; that is what was important. Denny was fine-boned and strong. He only weighed about 145 pounds but could handle any Duluth pack or canoe with ease. He wore a wrinkled cowboy hat and, along with is long grey beard, looked strikingly like a young Gabby Hayes, especially when he slapped his knee and giggled. He always wore an old hunting knife at his side. He cherished the knife because his father gave it to him many years ago. He liked to keep dry and did not enjoy plunging into the water. He usually donned rubber boots and rain gear at the first sign of rain. He usually hummed or sang with a fine baritone voice while he worked. His attitude was always good. He was the type of person who could get along with anyone. His mellow character was a buffer whenever anyone got emotionally down. Denny was our head mechanic and could fix anything mechanical or electrical. He loved to pull out his little bag of tools and fix things. He loved those challenges.

Denny liked to sneak a chew of tobacco now and then, but I never noticed him spitting out the juices. Curiosity finally overcame courtesy, and I finally asked him what became of the synthesized sap. He looked up, smiled, and, with a broad brown grin, said, "Swallow it." I did not ask any more questions. As far as I knew, nobody in the group smoked, so I was quite surprised to see Denny light up a stogie at the completion of the trip. He was especially health conscious, so I doubt it was a regular practice.

He enjoyed exercising, especially bicycle touring, so I assumed he was in good physical shape. I was quite surprised when he had a heart attack several months after the trip. He had an enlarged heart that none of us, even he, knew about. The heart attack would surely limit future outings.

Denny was also our only nonswimmer. He could not swim well but was wise enough to keep his life jacket on whenever he was near the water. Nevertheless, I kept a watchful eye on Denny.

I couldn't help thinking of his many great yarns whenever I thought of him. He was a great storyteller.

Next to Denny sat Lee Riegler and his petite wife, Marilyn. I spent a great deal of time with Lee in the past. We climbed a few mountains together in the Tetons, and that is an excellent way to get to know somebody. Lee was another fine-boned, hardworking lad who always tried and usually succeeded to overachieve. No task ever seemed impossible, and he was always willing to literally give you the shirt off his back. He loved to work hard, and I was amused at how he cranked on the canoe paddle and grit his teeth. It was like each stroke had to be stronger and harder than the last.

In the past, Lee had encountered several physical setbacks. He had a spinal fusion, neck problems, a knee operation, and most recently, a shoulder injury. He thought the shoulder injury might eliminate him from the trip, but after a secret emergency meeting, we all agreed that we should take him even if we would have to carry him. He had invested a great deal of time and energy into planning the voyage, so we felt he should go with us. He coyly accepted our proposal. He had no problems on the trip, but he almost wore us out with the pace he tried to set. We were glad we made the decision to take Lee.

It was apparent that Lee had other issues to mull over. He was going through his midlife stage and was anticipating a career change. Before the voyage began, he said he had a lot of things on his mind and had to work them out during the trip. All of us who were over thirty-five understood. He was a born-again Christian, and they often have the most difficulty making decisions because they always consider everyone else first and work under a higher order of rules. He eventually made career change from being the youth leader at the Rochester Covenant Church to a leadership role at the Mayo Clinic.

You can also learn a great deal about a person on an adventure odyssey like this. It is always interesting to observe people on a portage and what they select to carry. Lee would always survey the packs and equipment and choose the heaviest pack to carry. Then he would double back to fetch more. I would not be afraid to have Lee accompany me on any kind of excursion. His strength and stamina would always be welcome.

Then there was Bill Law Jr., sitting there alone, trying to have fun, but anxious to get home to his wife, Vicki. Bill was one of the most energetic and intense people I have ever met but also one of the most vibrant and colorful! Everything was always done with exaltation and flamboyance. He was fun to have around because he kept things lively. His enthusiasm and zest were impossible to contain and bubbled over on us.

Bill was well built, and dressed in a unique manner. He walked with bowed legs and would have made a great cowboy. He always wore a bright-Kelly-green hat that had two bills—one to shade his eyes and one to cover his neck. It was the type of hat big-game fishermen wore down in Florida. When he fished, he resembled a youthful Earnest Hemmingway. Whenever the weather was warm, he would strip down to his undershorts, which he usually wore inside out. He tended to favor the brand Fruit of the Loom. The label always proudly stuck out, so we could read it easily. After some discussion, we suspected that he reversed his shorts every day so he would have the feeling of wearing clean ones every day. We were never sure and never asked. We learned not to ask questions because there is always a certain amount of safety in ignorance. When the weather was cool, he would immediately put on the down coat that Vicki had sewn. I would watch him slip the jacket on and cuddle inside, relishing the thought that Vicki had constructed it with her delicate hands. This activity always warmed his body and his heart. I could tell because he always wore the silliest grin whenever he would don the coat.

It appeared he was always digging into his pack. We would just get underway when suddenly he would twist around in his canoe seat, flop on top of the equipment, unstrap his pack, open it up, and start throwing things out. It appeared whatever he wanted was always at the bottom. Denny, his partner, would sit in the stern and just shake his head and smile. The activity became predictable and annoying at first. Then it became humorous. Then it became hilarious. We would secretly bet on how long we would be underway before the excavation started.

Bill had some special concerns that added to his anxieties. He had not seen his wife for two weeks before the trip even started, and as the trip progressed, his loneliness multiplied. He spoke about Vicki often and wanted to call her on the phone at every opportunity, which was often impossible. When we sighted Oxford House (a Cree village about halfway), he began paddling so hard it was difficult for us to keep our lashed canoes going straight. He was also anxious to hear about his son who had a serious physical problem and was hospitalized frequently. We tried to empathize with him, but it is difficult when your healthy family is fresh in your mind.

Bill was also a medical doctor. He had just completed his residency at the Mayo Clinic and was going to join his father's practice in Tennessee. He commented often about problems involved with setting up practice, especially about getting a good nurse to help him. He was the professional's professional type, so I was sure the practice would be a success.

Nevertheless, we all enjoyed Bill's colorful personality and uncontainable enthusiasm, especially for fishing. He always had his rod in his hand. When we portaged, he always cast into the rapids in between carries. When we sailed, he trolled. Even when his canoe was swamped, he held his rod aloft like Moses's staff. I think he even slept with that rod. Whenever an unknowing fish struck at his lure and was seized, Bill would whoop and holler, and we would all laugh and giggle with contagious delight. I will miss Bill, but I will always remember him sitting in the bow of the canoe with his beacon-bright hat on, his dazzling-white shorts on, hiking boots on his feet, a vibrating rod in his hand, and his shouts of joy, all to the dismay of an unwary cross-eyed northern pike at the end of the line.

Then my eyes and thoughts moved to Steve Linquist, my canoeing partner. He was our youngest member at twenty-two, but his whitewater savvy was amazing. He would shift and crossbow stroke with ease. I enjoyed watching him move like a magician in the bow of the canoe. His analysis of the water current was uncanny too. Whenever we would stop to survey a rapid, his comments would impress me; I always concurred with his decision to run the rapids or not, and if we did run the water, what our route would be.

Steve was the quiet, slow-moving, and shy type. He never seemed to be in a hurry. I became aggravated on several occasions with his snaillike movement but finally learned to live with it and do whatever I could alone to prepare to embark. We capitalized on his shyness, and we teased him relentlessly about his many female friends back home. When we stopped at restaurants while on the road, he was also accused of flirting with any girls who might be in the establishment. The young Cree girls in the Hudson's Bay store at Oxford House found him especially handsome. They would point at him and giggle. We could not understand the language, but the gestures were communication enough.

Steve was a moderately sized man with a well-matured face for a lad so young. I would imagine the facial fissures were the result of his many outdoor excursions/outings in the torturous sun and inclement weather. He was quite muscular, agile, and dark complected with large white eyes and a brace of expansive incisors that gleamed when he smiled, which was often. When he laughed, it seemed to emanate from his toes, resulting in a husky rolling crescendo, beckoning others to join in. He took our teasing very well, so he was fun to have around.

I knew Steve well before the trip and got to know him even better during the voyage. We, along with Lee and sometimes Denny, rock climbed, cross-country skied, and bicycled together on many occasions. His skills, balance, and strength were a special gift. I always felt confident with Steve belaying or lead climbing.

Because Steve and I were canoe partners, we resided in the same tent. We would often stay up and chat, write in our journals, or check maps. One of Steve's nighttime activities, which irritated me to no end, was that he would pick at his toes just before going to sleep each night. The smell was excruciating, but I tried not to notice. I made sure I was the first to get up and start breakfast each morning; the toe-picking festivity was a great motivator. I did not care to have Steve's fingers prepare my breakfast.

After the toes were fully attended to, Steve would blow out his candle lantern, curl up in an angelic fetal position, and quickly doze away. I generally forced myself to stay awake to complete my journal writing, review the maps, and plan the next day's outing while Steve snored away. I was tempted to dig at my toes, thinking it might be therapeutic. I could not do it.

Steve had a distain for insects, and I found the only way he would move quickly was if the mosquitos and black flies were in pursuit. He always moved in a lackadaisical, viscous manner until insects appeared. Then he would become agitated and fluid. That was about the only time I was thankful for the many insects we encountered.

A canoer can always determine if the person is going to be a good paddling partner as soon as they board the canoe. If the person flops down in the seat and grabs the paddle by the throat like wringing the neck of a defenseless chicken, then the red flag of "rookie" needs to be mentally raised. But if the partner gingerly boards the canoe, feels the balance, and tries to tip the craft properly so it will track and respond as commanded, then one may be comforted to know that they are canoeing with a pro. As soon as Steve sat down in the canoe with me, I knew we would push water efficiently together. He looked back at me, looked at the load, sat down, jiggled the canoe, and dropped to his knees with the paddle poised in his hand in a businesslike manner. He was mentally prepared, and this made me confident. He always paddled with poise and resolve. He was a good partner, and I will miss him. We never canoed together again.

Now my thoughts turned to myself. It is impossible for a person to properly critique oneself, but I did have objectives for the trip that I thought were enlightening. And they were fulfilled. My major objective was to ensure that this expedition returned safely. Two wives asked me to be sure to return their husbands safely. I assured them that they, the men, had the skill and intellect necessary to complete the voyage. If we worked together and pooled our resources, I knew we would successfully complete the voyage and have an enjoyable, rewarding experience. Keeping the group together would be the key to success, and with six individualists, the task might be difficult.

At one of our first meetings, we discussed leadership. Our conclusion was that an overall leader (bourgeois) would have to be selected to make all the final decisions. This person would have to take the responsibility of making sure all prevoyage tasks were completed and of making all the difficult decisions while en route. Whoever was to be selected would have the difficult task of giving orders. I was selected to this unamiable task. I accepted the position with reluctance because I knew I might become unpopular. People who give orders are seldom popular. I asked for and received their assurance for support and cooperation.

Each voyager reminded me of a section of the Hayes River.

Mike reminded me of the final section of the Hayes—the broad, flat, and rolling length of water that reached from Gods River to the Hudson Bay. The water was powerful and full of wisdom after the long journey from the proximal to the distal end. The water was quiet but fast. Power, calmness, and wisdom with little noise or turbidity—that was Mike.

Denny was more like the first section of the river—a section of water that carefully picked and chose its meandering route through the islands and trees. The river at this stretch was calculating and yet anxious to move. It was careful and yet willing to take reasonable risks. It was quiet and yet rippled on occasion, just like Denny.

Lee was like the rapids through which we passed preceding the Swampy Lake entrance—a section with a great deal of crashing power yet with sanctuaries of eddies strategically located behind the boulders and islands. It was a carefree section of water which offered involvement and thrills while providing safety and an attitude of caring. That was Lee—strong, full of fun, and always offering care.

Bill also reminded me of moving water, but he was more like Horseshoe Falls—noticeably quiet on top but crashing with noise and irreversible agitation at the bottom. The difficult aspect of falls is that they are unpredictable until the crest is reached. Then the noise and power enlighten emotions. Bill was the same way: strong, noisy, and yet exhilarating to watch and admire. Bill always played hard and rested hard just like the Horseshoe Falls and the pool that rested below.

No question about it, Steve was like the deep channels we passed through. Although the river narrowed in the channel and water velocity decreased, the river became deeper. In the channels, the water would be deep, dark, silent, and mysterious. That was Steve. His quietness and deep thoughts were like those channels.

Now the voice of the river no longer serenaded us. Instead, there was the throb of the jukebox blaring uncontrollably. The air was no longer crisp and alive. Now there was cigarette smoke inhaled by innocent lungs. But we were together for our final goodbyes in this concrete abode, and we were going to make the best of it. I could not wait to sink my incisors into one of those greasy pizza wedges.

I thought about the contrasts we lived in. Here we were, about to eat pizza at the local establishment. Just two days before, we were tired, hungry, worried, and wet. Now we were safe, dry, smelling good, with our loved ones, and about to have Bill's favorite pizza.

Like each section of the Hayes, I will miss each voyager. Each one, like each section of the river, collectively made a valuable change in my memory cells. I will always remember their laughs, shouts of joy, and smiles as a hearty group of men who challenged the Hayes River odyssey.

Another aspect of most celebrations are sorrowful departures. I never saw some of the voyagers again. After toiling in the wilderness with these great lads, it was difficult to say goodbye. I hope they and their kin enjoy my recounting our odyssey.

Chapter 2

In the Beginning

Coming together is a beginning; keeping together is progress; working together is success
—Edward Everett Hale

It was a typical Minnesota winter in Rochester with snow, ice, and cold! Suddenly, one evening, Lee and Steve rang the doorbell. I opened it, and they anxiously jumped in the doorway without invitation, hyperventilating with excitement. They stomped the sticky December snow from their boots and kicked them off with the obvious intention of staying awhile. They each had a sheepish look on their face, so I knew something was up and that I was going to be part of it. I acted defensive, curious, and cautious. When one's rock climbing partners visit with that wide-eyed look on their faces, you know you are going to be included in an adventure. They gingerly meandered to the couch and made themselves comfortable—again, without invitation—crossed their legs, and looked down at the floor as if they had a secret to tell me. But Lee soon came right to the point of the visit as they began to extol our next outdoor trek.

"How would you like to run the Hayes River to Hudson Bay?" Lee blurted as he raised his head.

Steve slowly raised his head too and smiled.

I had to sit down to absorb the surprising proposal. Then I also cast my eyes to the floor in hopes that they would not see my anxiety. I had planned to go climbing in the Tetons again that summer, but the offer seemed enticing.

Before I could utter any response, Lee continued: "Steve and I have been thinking about getting a group together to run the Hayes, and we want you to be a part of the expedition."

Steve smiled.

I began to squirm. I felt like a marauding hungry trout patrolling a mountain stream.

Lee just launched a number 24 midge to this hungry cutthroat trout.

Steve smiled.

This tempted but wary trout was now rising to the fly for inspection and introspection.

Lee quickly added with a slight rod twitch, "It will be about a four-week trip, and I know you'll enjoy running the miles of whitewater rapids."

Steve continued to smile.

The Hayes River is a historic waterway in norther Manitoba, Canada, utilized by the First Nations People and voyageurs to transport valuable pelts, especially beaver hides, and to obtain trade goods in return. Rivers in Canada were like our modern-day superhighways or rail systems to transport materials and people. The First Nations People first plied birchbark canoes up and down the river, but the Europeans introduced the sailing York boats and later, steam vessels for faster and more efficient transport. The rapids and falls remained as obstacles, so portages were used to circumvent these challenges. The Hayes originates in Molson Lake and traverses northwest to Hudson Bay, some three hundred miles, through a series of lakes, rapids, and falls. This sounded like a time-warping experience.

They both knew that this trout had just leaped upon the innocent fly, but now the trout (me) needed to be played and landed. I said, "I will have to think about it and talk it over with Donna."

They knew I was hooked, but this fish would have to be played awhile at another opportune time; the caught fish had to be run against the drag for a while. Besides, a trek of this magnitude requires proper spousal protocol.

Steve smiled.

Then they stoically stood like soldiers at attention, nodded, and departed. I grasped the doorknob tightly and bid them goodbye as I trembled with excitement. After talking the proposal over with Donna (I am sure she overheard the dialogue while she was in the kitchen), she leaned around the corner and nodded with approval. After checking my summer calendar, I phoned Lee and surrendered. Trout landed! I am sure Lee felt proud with such a hefty creel.

So the trip was gendered. Denny, who was another climbing partner, soon joined in, and we were now four strong. The word went out that we might need some medical expertise. Bill Law, who was a member of my and Lee's church, quickly volunteered. Bill contacted Mike Heinle, and we were a complete voyager brigade ready to push and pull water.

We held our first meeting at my house. After proper introductions, we settled down to business. I handed out a sheet for each voyager to fill out. This included the name, address, telephone number, emergency phone number, physical limitations, allergies, and canoeing/outdoor experiences of each. I wanted to know more about each person. We also discussed the rationale for the excursion. We needed to know what each member's expectations were. This was also an opportunity for an introspective analysis. The discussion was enlightening. We knew we had a lot of preparations to contend with, so we decided to meet monthly to keep on task. Preparation often determines the success of any venture.

The second meeting was held on January 13, 1983. Everyone was ready and willing to accept responsibilities and eager to do their part, so it looked like the expedition would be easy to organize.

Lee volunteered to be the secretary/treasurer, which was good to hear. I knew he was a good organizer and skilled with handling funds—an important aspect of any organization. Lee was also selected as the "dry leader" and in charge of all overland logistics. This included the road route, the railway tickets for the return trip, and contacting the outfitter for the airdrop arrangements into Molson Lake, the start of the voyage.

We enlightened Steve that we decided to enlist his truck and that we would pay for the necessary fuel. Steve smiled—usually an affirmative answer, but we were never sure. The truck's engine was noisy but powerful, and we felt if it has puffed through 120,000 miles, it could gasp through another 1,000. New tires were procured and mounted as a precaution. We did not have faith in the baldies he had on the vehicle. Lee had a canoe rack welded up for his heavy-duty trailer that was in great shape. We felt Denny could find enough wire, pop rivets, and sheet metal screws to hold Steve's truck—the yellow snow pile—together on the road trip to and from Gilam, Canada.

Any extended excursion needs medical expertise, and we were lucky because we had two doctors! Bill and Mike would act as out medics. They took the task seriously and synthesized two elaborate first aid kits that contained everything from forceps to scissors to Band-Aids to sutures to splints to gauze and other essentials. They even packed the necessary materials to temporarily fill teeth. Everything in duplicate was stored in two white-painted waterproof surplus ammunition boxes for visibility. The kits would travel in separate canoes, lest one canoe capsized and lost. I felt we were in great medical hands. They had served in emergency rooms, and their experiences and expertise were comforting.

I was selected as the "bushwa," or overall leader. My major assignment was to coordinate efforts of all other leaders to enhance continuity and reduce duplication. I felt guilty with my soft assignment, but I knew it would become more difficult as plans progressed and paddling ensued. I also volunteered to be the historian and record all significant happenings on the trip. This text is the result of that effort.

The third meeting was held at Lee's house on February 24. It was a dark, cold night, but we had no problem concentrating on reporting our responsibilities. Lee had procured a wealth of information from the Canadian government and the Manitoba Department of Tourism, which he presented along with our painful financial status. We were enlightened but now poorer. Mike and Bill entertained us with emergency medical demonstrations using their first aid kits. We found the suture demonstrations on an orange especially informative, entertaining, and a great safety incentive. We agreed to be especially careful!

Mike and Bill also reviewed, at length, CPR with us. They felt all members of the crew should be versed in this valuable life-saving technique, which, if we were lucky, we would never have to use. They also surveyed the group as to our fitness and physical preparedness. Two things they especially wanted to know were…when we had our last tetanus shot and who wore false teeth. I was the only one with a masquerading incisor attached to a small palate—the result of an old baseball injury. Our thoughts then turned to equipment, so we planned to have the next meeting at my house to discuss equipment. Steve volunteered to be the "wet leader," and he would be responsible for all on water logistics. He would have to make the critical decisions regarding when to paddle or when to sail the large lakes, when to run rapids or when to portage, and where to camp. All were critical to safety and success. Steve also procured and waterproofed all topographical maps. There was one complete set for each canoe. He would have to do most of map and compass navigation—a task Lee and I would assist him with.

Mike insisted, to our delight, to be the menu manager and chef, and a great one he turned out to be. Disappointing meals ruin any otherwise joyous excursion. Bill volunteered to assist him in this arduous task. The menus had to be planned carefully to provide adequate caloric content, to reduce the total supply weight, and to add enjoyment to the trip. Mike and Bill also had to dehydrate, package, label, and equally distribute all the food among the three canoes.

Denny was the equipment troubleshooter and would analyze and repair mechanical menaces—something he excelled at. One of our major concerns was the mode of overland transportation. We decided to use Steve's old suburban van. It was a rusted-out hulk that was once white and now looked like a big pile of yellow snow. The doorposts were rusted off the frame, so Denny wired most of the doors on. Where sheet metal was threatening to precipitate, he fastened with pop rivets or sheet metal screws. It was not pretty. But the motor was sound. As a result of the repairs, none of the doors opened except for the driver's door. To enter and exit, we had to crawl through the rolled-down windows. By the end of the overland trek, I felt more like a mole than a voyager.

The equipment meeting was at 6:30 p.m. on March 3. Spring was approaching, and we were getting anxious. This was a low-budget adventure, so some equipment had to be purchased, some shared, and others borrowed. One thing for sure, all equipment we would take would be used. We did not want to haul and portage any trivia because trivia gets heavy.

Our vessels, the canoes, were one of the most important pieces of equipment. Bill, Denny, and Mike volunteered to purchase canoes because they would like to have one after the voyage. My sixteen-foot Old Town was not considered because it would not adequately hold the necessary load. Seventeen-foot aluminum Grummans were selected for the task because they were economical, durable, easy to repair, and buoyant. They also had the important keel.

The development of the Grumman canoe is an interesting story in itself. Mark Neuzil and Norman Sims authored *Canoes: A Natural History in North America* (University of Minnesota Press), which describes the evolution of this popular canoe. During the Second World War, the Grumman company made the famed F4F Wildcat and F6F Hellcat fighters. Thousands were built to help win WWII. But after the war, the company had the aluminum sheet metal stretching, fabrication machinery, and aluminum material with no orders for additional aircraft. The Army and Navy (no Air Force yet) cancelled all remaining plane orders.

Grummand F4F Wildcat

About the same time, Grumman's chief tool engineer, William Hoffman, an avid outdoorsman, took a canoe trip to the Adirondacks in a heavy canvas-covered wood canoe (popular at the time) and thought an aluminum canoe would be lighter, sturdier, and cheaper. After making and testing several prototypes, they began production in 1944 in the company's bowling alley. By 1946, the company had orders for more than 10,000 canoes at $157 each and became the nation's largest canoe producer, manufacturing 33,000 canoes annually by 1970s. They were manufactured by riveting two mirrored sides together with a keel, which was important to us because a keel helps to track the canoe on flat water.

Canoes are really "freedom machines," like bicycles. They do not inhale valuable oxygen and exhale smog. They are quiet and tidy. The original canoes were dugout logs, like we used in the Congo or the birchbark variety developed by the Native Americans or First Nations People. Old Town and a few other companies developed the cedar canvas-covered canoe that was popular for many years. I loved them because they were organic and vocal, made with nature's living material, and groaned or murmured with each stroke while slicing through the water. But they were not very durable in the rapids. It was rare to find one without a few broken ribs and patches. The aluminum canoe was a wonderful answer, but some considered them ugly. I remember Sig Olson, the well-known north country canoer and author, referring to canoers portaging aluminum canoes as metal turtles! Nevertheless, the Grummans were the selected vehicles.

Next were the important paddles that needed to be light and durable. Heavy paddles tend to wear down the paddlers. We measured for paddles, and Steve ordered custom-made paddles from a new Twin Cities firm, Bending Branches, and they performed admirably. At the time, the fledgling company made them in a garage. We stowed away an extra aluminum-shafted paddle in each canoe in case of brakeage or loss.

The Mounties reminded us that history of the river is that one canoe would be lost and one member would break an arm or leg! We decided to replace any broken or lost group equipment from our general fund. This policy would cover the cost of a canoe for the individual who made the initial purchase. We surmised that we would probably lose a canoe, but our prognostication proved incorrect because all we lost were a washrag while I was taking a Hays River bath, Mike's knife-sharpening hone and rod tip, Lee's sierra cup while he answered nature's call, and about twenty-five lures Bill sacrificed to the rocks in pursuit of fish.

I fabricated a list that included everything I could think of that might be needed and functional by gleaning through my old logs, journals (which I always keep), and lists used for other excursions. From these, I carefully selected items that were light, portable, and functional. I itemized the equipment into categories such as camera equipment, fishing equipment, group equipment, individual canoe equipment, and personal items. The personal category included items we each would need and offered some flexibility as to personal desires. In spite of my brainstorming, the group thought of things I missed that were incorporated into the list. We tried to share and improvise as much as possible to save costs. Items that were used often or used for several functions were especially valuable.

We each brought camera equipment except for Mike; he said he would duplicate copies after the trip from our many slides/pictures. Bill decided to take pictures instead of slides. Many of them were great shots. Steve burned up most film and, consequently, was the group's unofficial photographer.

We used Denny's, Lee's, and my tents. Steve ordered necessary Duluth packs even though some of us already had packs. I brought a large 10' by 12" nylon fly to cook under during the rain and to use as our sail when we crossed the foreboding lakes. We needed something to cook on, so I welded together a portable cooking grate that would fold up and pack easily. Other items were purchased or scrounged up by the group. The equipment list can be found in the appendix, and our equipment selection must have been adequate because everything worked fine. Now we looked forward to our shakedown cruise.

Chapter 3

The Shakedown Cruise

*For the things we have to learn before we can
do them, we learn by doing them.*

—Aristotle

The shakedown cruise was scheduled for the Memorial Day weekend, so we would have enough time to travel to some waterway challenging enough to test our abilities. We selected the historic and scenic Brule River in Northern Wisconsin for our encounter because it was one of the few rivers with large-enough rapids and was long enough for our canoeing assessment. The Brule River is a well-known trout and steelhead fishing river. I had fly-fished in the famous river as a graduate student at the University of Wisconsin in Superior. I had fallen hopelessly in love with the river while fly-fishing on the weekends, and the romance progressed. I always wanted to embrace the river from Stone's Bridge to Lake Superior with my canoe and fish in its pools, riffles, and rapids. It looked like my fantasies would finally materialize with this cruise.

The river was a major trading route for the early voyageurs. They would paddle up the river from Lake Superior and traverse a short but hilly portage to the St. Croix River, which ran downstream to the Mississippi River. I learned that many of the voyageurs who skipped along these rapids may have also floated the Hayes River, our destination. Our anticipation grew.

Donna, my wife, Josie, my faithful springer spaniel, and I arrived early on Friday night to our humble camper on Lake George in Bayfield County, Wisconsin. I hurriedly turned on the electricity and gas while Donna hauled in supplies, and Josie ran down to the dock to check the water, take a quick dip, and look for careless sunfish. Mike and Margaret, his wife, arrived shortly after. They limped in with Mike's antiquated Gremlin with the shiny new Grumman strapped to the top. Somehow the combination did not seem to go together, but it didn't matter. Mike bounced out, decked out in the new Gore-Tex ensemble that Margaret stitched together. Mike and his attire seemed to buffer the effects of the car and canoe clash. Lee and Steve arrived with most of the equipment stuffed in Lee's '70s Oldsmobile. They pulled in late, but I knew it was them because I could see Steve's teeth glowing in the dark! Lee owned the lot next door, so I knew he knew the way. Bill arrived shortly after with his canoe draped over his cancerous Datsun. His new canoe and rusty car were also a paradox in motion. As usual, Bill was ready to go. Denny had a little trouble finding the elusive retreat, so we formulated a search and rescue team. But he finally arrived before we could activate the search. The group was now intact, and there was an air of excitement and anticipation. We were looking forward to whitewater and canoeing work tomorrow.

We excitedly chatted into the late night but finally decided to prepare for tomorrow with needed sleep. Donna and I slept in our camper while Bill, Denny, and Steve slumbered in Denny's dome tent and Mike and Lee bedded in in Lee's Timberline tent.

I awoke at 4:30 a.m. to the revving of Lee's Oldsmobile's trembling exhaust pipes. During the night, he had been viciously attacked by our local predators—the wood ticks. He scurried to the nearby campground where he took a shower and deticked his innocent body. It was an uncomfortable night for him, especially with Mike snoring through the ordeal. I could not sleep anymore, so I slipped out of bed, trying not to awake Donna, grabbed my spinning rod, and snuck down to the lake. I quietly launched my Old Town canoe into the lake and fished for bass. I only caught and released one "keeper" size.

Everyone was up and milling about by 7:00 a.m. Bill and Mike had a crackling fire going, and our first experimental meal was offered. It was great. Great cooks make good food. Good food helps make a good outing. Things were already looking up.

Any exploratory group needs to know the strengths and weaknesses of the individual participants, and therefore, a shakedown cruise was planned. The swimming assessment was the first trial. Donning our swimsuits, we jumped into the frigid water of the lake and stroked hard to the isthmus across the lake. Denny wore a life jacket, and the girls monitored us in canoes. Denny confessed that he was not a strong swimmer, and Steve didn't particularly like swimming either. Then we practiced our paddling strokes, weaving around milk-bottle buoys mimicking river boulders in the lake. Most people erroneously think the sternman does all the steering, but the bowman actually has a better view of potential hazards in the rapids and can guide the canoe quicker with a draw or crossbow stroke sideways, eluding rocks or boulders. We exchanged positions and partners several times to develop empathy for our partner and develop essential communicative and paddling skills, which are critical in maintaining a proper canoe attitude in water, going straight downriver and not sliding sideways into disaster.

Now it was time to check our life-saving skills. I purposely glided my canoe into the deeper water, flipped my cane, and gritted my teeth as I waited facedown in the icy water. Without prompting, Steve, my partner, wisely pushed the submerged vessel to Lee and Denny's canoe while Mike and Bill glided quickly to my side and turned me faceup to breathe. It was no time before Denny and Lee had our canoe emptied by sliding our upside-down canoe crossways across their canoe gunnels and back into the water right-side up while Mike and Bill had me hauled into their canoe with some effort. It was not an easy task because I tried to be as limp as possible. Mike later said it was like trying to load a big bunch of Jell-O! The comment was not complimentary, but that is the way an unconscious person would normally behave. I was glad to see that the crew could rescue a canoe and victim efficiently.

One of Mike's lunches was bolted down with gusto, and we loaded the canoes for the Brule River's challenge. The upper part of the Brule is timid, so I did not anticipate any mishaps. And it would be a good section for us to familiarize ourselves with the canoe's maneuverability and our partner's strokes and movements. Only riffles were glissaded while artificial flies and spinners flew from the silver hulls. Bill caught a nice brown trout, which he kept. All the other victims to our imitation morsels were gently returned to their aquatic abodes. The girls picked us up at Highway B Bridge where they were also trying to catch trout. It seemed strange to watch Donna casting to the colorful rascals. We had a great time and worked well together. We chatted noisily as we rumbled back to lake George between the towering pines, anticipating Mike's delightful meal, a friendly campfire, and tomorrow's more treacherous challenge of the lower Brule caldrons.

We were all quietly up early and checking equipment over carefully because we knew we would be fighting heavier water. This stretch of water would fully judge our abilities. The girls dropped us off where they picked us up the day before and scampered down to Highway 2 where they would pick us up in the afternoon. We cascaded down the riffles and the larger rapids past the HH Bridge, then over the Mays Ledges and falls, and down through "rocky roller coasters," past fly-fishermen with mouths agape. We ran all the rapids and did not think we needed to practice portaging. Steve became concerned because we were not checking rapids as often and as closely as we had planned. He was concerned about the condition of the canoes among the blocking boulders. He was correct, so rapids of consequence were then carefully surveyed before being run. The girls picked us up, and we were soon joyously driving back to George Lake to pack and return to Rochester, confident now with our newly procured whitewater success. I loved the Brule River since the first time I experienced its rapids while in college, and it became a familiar venue for my fly-fishing excursions. We knew the Brule would not measure up to the Hayes, but it was the best nearby rapids available. We all got wet, but it was a successful group learning experience. We felt comfortable and confident working together and all maintained a safe attitude. Safety is always paramount. It would be foolish to not try to plan out any catastrophe.

But we knew we had a lot of work to do yet. The food needed to be packed, and everything had to be doubly checked and weighed before we could depart. I felt the pressure of time. I had a lot to do before the departure. I had to complete teaching summer school classes and lead the BWCA trip for my ecology class. But I was sure everyone felt pressured.

Chapter 4

Final Preparations

By failing to prepare, you are preparing to fail.
—Benjamin Franklin

We finally met a couple of days before loading equipment at Lee's house. They had a large basement and garage, and we knew Marilynn, his wife, would be patient with a noisy brigade of busy voyagers. Denny was soon busy sewing up the canoe skirts on his rattling machine. Mike and Bill, murmuring in the corner, were working on the food menus and packs. The rest of us drilled holes into the canoe gunwales and fastened the snaps for the skirts. The basement looked as though a freight train had derailed with equipment and tools scattered in organized disarray. It was chaotic but humming with efficiency.

We knew we would encounter daily rain and thunderstorms and run unforgiving rapids, so we had to prepare ourselves and our equipment. We purchased reinforced orange (for visibility) plastic tarps and large snaps to make splash guards or skirt covers to help keep as much rain and the Hayes River from invading our canoes. Denny lugged his sewing machine to the work session in Lee's garage and proceeded to manufacture the splash guards while Lee and I drilled and placed the snap units into the canoe gunwales and covers. Bill and Mike toiled on the menu and first aid kits. Lee and I tended the nested cook kit and grate that I had welded up.

Dennis sewing the spray skirts for the canoes

Bill and Mike pondering the cooking equipment dilemma

Lee and Steve fastening the snaps for the spray skirts

Individual equipment needs

Everything was weighed, including us, to insure equal distribution of material mass among canoes. Our pack weights ranged from Denny's 80-pound pack to bills 103-pounder. Lee was the lightest voyager at 145 pounds, so he was matched with Mike's 208 pounds.

Obviously, Lee would paddle in the bow. Mike and Lee carried the lighter 73-pound group pack while the other two packs were 100 pounds each. Mike and Lee still ended up with most total weight of 627 pounds. The total weight of everyone and everything was 2,045 pounds! We were now at a ton strong and prepared to paddle and sail. We were ready. The only tasks remaining were to kiss the ladies goodbye, say a prayer for safety, and crawl into Steve's old van—the pile of yellow snow—and depart.

The team packing, preparing to leave

Chapter 5

Henry Hudson and His Travels

A sea setting us upon the ice has brought us close to danger.
—Henry Hudson

During the fifteenth to seventeenth centuries, many European monarchs and businesspeople were obsessed with finding a northern route from Europe to Asia to capitalize on the riches and opportunities of the Far East. There were several explorers in quest of this tedious and dangerous goal. But Henry was probably one of the least successful explorers even though a river, bay, and strait are named after him.

In 1607, the English Muscovy Company asked Henry to find a route across the North Pole to China. He sailed north from England with his crew up the coast of Greenland, but ice stopped him. Then in 1608, he tried heading along the north coast of Russia without success again. So in 1609, he tried to go over Norway, Sweden, and Finland, but his crew threatened mutiny. And he decided to cross the Atlantic to the American coast. He thought he found the elusive Northwest Passage, only to discover it was a large freshwater river later named the Hudson River. His final journey was in 1610 where he headed further north and discovered the large bay that now bears his name—Hudson Bay. But it didn't turn out well. The ship froze in the ice, and Hudson and his crew were forced to spend the winter frozen in the ice of the bay. The following year, 1611, his crew mutinied and set Henry, his young son, and seven loyal crew members adrift in a small boat in the bay, never to be heard from again. Alas, Henry is still someplace in the clutches of the bay named after him.

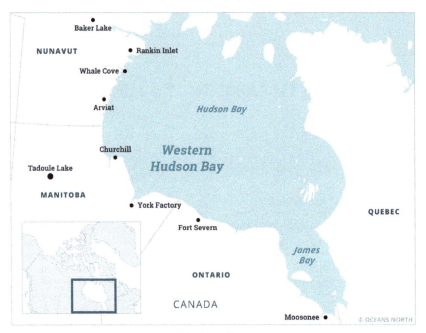

Hudson Bay
Note the location of York Factory

Chapter 6

The Hayes River

Wild rivers are earth's renegades, defying gravity, dancing to their own tunes, resisting the authority of humans, always chipping away, and eventually always winning.
—Richard Bangs and Christian Kallen (*River Gods*)

The historic three-hundred-mile Hayes River in Manitoba, Canada, flows from Molson Lake, northeast of Lake Winnipeg, to Hudson Bay at York Factory. It features whitewater rapids, large lake systems, waterfalls, deep valleys, and gorges as well as tidal flats with a mean discharge of twenty-one thousand cubic feet per second and a drainage basin covering forty-two square miles. The Hayes is the longest naturally flowing river in Manitoba with no dams or development to mar its course.

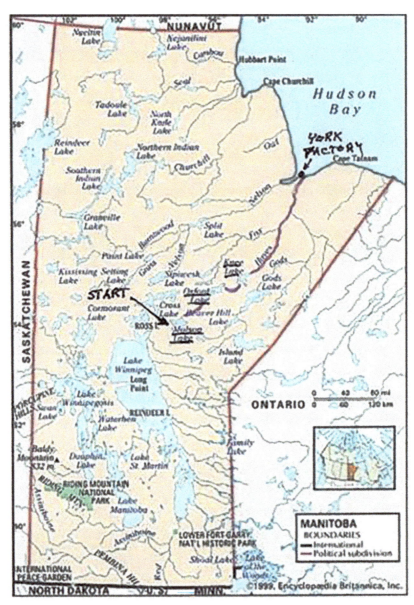

Manitoba with Hayes River route

The course of the river begins at Molson Lake at an elevation of 725 feet. Then it flows north and northeast to Robinson Lake, about 10 miles. Across Robinson Lake is Robinson Falls and the wrenching mile-long Robinson portage, the longest portage between Hudson Bay and Edmonton. Hill Gates, a mile-long narrow gorge, is a short distance to be contended with, and beyond this, the river cuts across Logan Lake and passes the settlement of Wetikoweskwattam to Opiminegoka Lake. There, it flows northeast again to Windy Lake and over Wipanipanis Falls to the large Oxford Lake, about fifty miles from Molson Lake (its source). Then it flows past Oxford House, a Cree village, and out of Oxford Lake over Trout Falls to Knee Lake. From Knee Lake, the river passes through a series of percolating rapids via several confusing channels and widens into Swampy Lake, about 120 miles northeast of Molson Lake and 150 miles from Hudson Bay. This stretch includes the most difficult part of the river including a 50-mile stretch where it loses five-sevenths of its elevation and one-sixth of its length. From Swampy Lake, it runs through constant rapids and past an important landmark, Brassy Hill, rising 459 feet above the river. It continues northeast through a small canyon for 62 miles, passing over Whitemud Falls and Berwick Falls, eventually joining Gods River at an elevation of 79 feet and finally reaching its mouth at Hudson Bay, just south of Nelson River. Along the way, several smaller tributaries flow into the Hayes. Sections of the river originally had names of their own.

Canoeing the pristine river, one might see a myriad of wildlife, including polar bears, wolverines, woodland caribou, the ivory gull, bald eagles, and moose as well as aquatic inhabitants like the sturgeon, brook trout, whitefish, pike, walleye, and beluga whales. Towering spruce and tamarack dominate the shoreline along with alders. The shorelines of the river and lakes are not interrupted with cabins or resorts, giving the river system a genuine primitive flavor. On June 11, 2006, the river was designated as a Canadian Heritage River, and at the confluence of the Gods and Hayes Rivers is a marker to a young canoe guide that died at twenty-two years of age. In a nearby grove of trees, there is supposed to be a waterproof can for people to leave a message, which we never found.

The river has a storied history. It was first used by the First Nations people, and the river is punctuated with numerous pictographs at ancient rocky campsites. It became an important waterway in the development of Canada when the Europeans arrived. The river was named in 1684 for Sir James Hayes, a Hudson's Bay Company charter member and secretary to Prince Rupert, by French trader/explorer Pierre Radisson. At the mouth of the Hayes, in the same year, the HBC established York Factory, which served as HBC's North American headquarters until 1957. During this time, it was the main water route between York Factory and Norway House in the interior of the continent for explorers, traders, voyageurs, settlers, and now paddlers, like us.

A HAYES RIVER ODYSSEY

Hayes River historical map

Chapter 7

To Canada

The pain of parting is nothing to the joy of meeting again.
—Charles Dickens

Departure

July 9, 1983

Now was the time to say goodbye. We stowed the packs in the bottom of the trailer and covered them with a waterproof tarp. Above, the three canoes were lofted onto the rack and fastened. We were anxious yet pensive to roll, not really knowing what was ahead. The next day, July 9, 1983, we gathered at Lee's house in a fellowship circle with our wives, families, and a few friends in a solemn departing ceremony climaxed with a prayer and tearful embracing goodbyes. This would be the last time we would see or communicate with our loved ones for some time because there was no way to communicate while on the river. We climbed through the windows of the suburban yellow pile of snow and disembarked, rumbling north on Highway 52.

The trip to the Canadian border was uneventful with the voyagers taking turns driving, sleeping, and checking the load with each stop, but we were concerned that the border guard would order us to unload everything for inspection. It was dark and extremely late when we stopped at the border, and the yawning border guard stumbled to the vehicle. Steve rolled down the driver side window and smiled. The guard inquired about our plans and destination and if we had any handguns. We had no handgun and revealed such, but we did take a .270 Remington pump rifle that a friend insisted on our taking (he wanted to be part of the excursion). I knew the rifle would not ward off any polar bear we might encounter but would make a lot of repulsive noise. After we confessed our plans of our Hudson Bay expedition, the guard smiled, shook his head with a sympathetic grin, and benevolently waved us on.

Canada Travel Requirements

NOTE:

Be advised that Canadian travel requirements are now more stringent than when we crossed the border in route to our Hayes River Odyssey. When we crossed the border in the '80's it was as easy and simple as visiting your neighbor. With the onset of COVID-19, firearm restrictions and other issues, care must be taken when crossing the border lest the group be stymied.

Keep the following in mind:
- Canada is our sister country, but nevertheless, it is a different country and travelers must abide by the host countries rules. You may not like the rules, but remember, *when in Rome do as romans do.*
- When crossing the border be polite and attentive. Being rude to the border guard could result with a total search of all equipment. I have seen this happen!
- Have all the required paperwork handy to present. Don't be fumbling around for requested documents.
- Do not carry any firearms, contraband, alcohol, or control substances. It will probably be found resulting with an embarrassing episode or fine. Enjoy the wilderness!
- It is always a good idea to carry your passport and driver license w/picture.

COVID-19 restrictions in Canada are more aggressively enforced than the more lenient American restrictions and must be followed to cross the border. Before venturing North, one should visit "Canadian Travel Requirements" first because changes are always occurring.

Presently the requirements for COVID-19 include:

1. Check if you qualify as a fully vaccinated traveler:
   - Have received at least 2 doses of a COVID-19 vaccine accepted for travel, a mix of 2 accepted vaccines or at least 1 dose of the Janssen/Johnson & Johnson vaccine
   - Have received your second dose at least 14 calendar days before you enter Canada
   - Have no signs or symptoms of COVID-19
   - Have ArriveCAN receipt with letter A, I, or V beside your name by <u>uploading proof of vaccination in ArriveCAN</u> (from the website)
2. Checklist of what you need to have ready at the border:
   - ArriveCAN receipt with letter A, I, or V beside the vaccinated traveler's name.
   - Proof of vaccination that was uploaded into ArriveCAN (original or paper copy)
   - Prepare for arrival testing if randomly selected
   - Travel document entered in ArriveCAN (e.g. passport)

Wabowden

We drove hard to Wabowden, where we would board two airplanes that Lee had ordered to drop us off on Molson Lake at the start of the Hayes River. We finally made it to Wabowden at 7:00 p.m. The planes were fueled and ready, but George, the head pilot, was not there! After anxious searching and calling around, he was discovered at home watching baseball via USA satellite. George proved to be an okay guy, though. He invited us to use his office as sleeping quarters until the next day when we would leave. The office, however, was full of hungry mosquitos waiting to devour innocent American paddlers. But we fought back by applauding them to death before retiring to a sound sleep. At 10:00 p.m., we strode a short distance to George's wife's café where we feasted on homemade pierogi with greasy bacon, gravy, and cream sauce. What a treat! I thought and reminisced how often I had the precious Czechoslovakian dish my mom would make for special occasions like Easter and Christmas when I lived as a boy in central Wisconsin on a small farm. Mom could only speak broken English but was a great old-world cook.

We stopped at the RCMP office to register our itinerary and disclose our plans. After discussing our voyage to the Mountie, he made an ominous remark. While looking down at the maps we provided, he tilted his head to the side, looked at us out of the corner of his eye, and proclaimed, "Be careful. The water is the highest this spring than it has been for many years. The water has invaded much of the forest." Then he topped his warning with the ominous comment, "The history of the river is that you will lose one canoe, and a member will break a leg or arm."

He concluded with the typical Canadian exclamation "eh." We knew campsites would be at a premium and that the rapids would be higher than we figured.

Team loading equipment on the planes

Itinerary

The plan was to have planes drop us off on Molson Lake. We would then run the Hayes to York Factory (a fur processing mecca a couple of hundred years ago) and have jet boats pick us up and take us up the Nelson River to Gilam, Manitoba, where we would board a train (boxcar reserved for canoes and equipment) back to Wabowden and then drive back to Rochester. Well, that was the plan, which had to be altered later. We originally considered starting at Lake Winnipeg. But we all had tight schedules, so we decided to start at Molson Lake, the source of the Hayes.

After Steve (wet leader) and I briefed the group on possible campsites along the river and reviewed our itinerary, we did some final pack adjustments and tumbled into our sleeping bags. It was a hot, stuffy night with an occasional mosquito singing in our ears. It was 12:30 a.m., and we were excited and chatting like children about tomorrow's flight.

Chapter 8

Delight of Flight

It's only when you're flying above it that you realize how incredible the Earth really is.
—Phillippe Perrin

Lee had ordered airplanes to drop us into Molson Lake, the start of our odyssey, and they were marvelous machines. The de Havilland planes are of Canadian origin with the Beaver first developed as the workhorse and the Otter later as the freighter. The Cessna 185 was also used for the lighter loads.

deHavilland Beaver

Wikipedia has provided the following information about the planes: The Beaver is a single-engine, high-wing, propeller-driven short takeoff and landing aircraft. It was primarily operated as a bush plane and used for cargo, passengers, aerial applications, and civil aviation duties and made its maiden voyage August 16, 1947. There were 1,657 made, and many are still in service. Although, production ceased in 1967. It is thirty feet and three inches long with a wingspan of forty-eight feet. It can cruise at 142.92 miles per hour with a range of 455 miles and can haul 1,500 pounds of cargo. Many consider the Beaver as the best bush plane ever! Several companies still make parts for the endearing craft that still graces the skies over Canada, Alaska, and many other countries. The radial engine Beaver was replaced by a turboprop model in 1963.

deHavilland Otter

The larger Otter, a stretched-out Beaver, is a high-wing, single-engine, short takeoff and landing plane also and made its maiden flight on December 12, 1951. It has a wingspan of fifty-eight feet and ten inches and is forty-one feet and ten inches long. It was conceived to be capable of performing the same roles as the Beaver but is larger for greater capacity. Although it can hold eleven passengers, it is most important as a transport plane for delivering goods. The radial engines of both planes have a distinctive sound, almost like a flathead Ford. You can tell when they fly overhead. They are no longer built. The DHC-6 has taken over, a twin-engine turboprop model.

Inside our de Havilland Otter, door to cockpit, and Tony, the Otter pilot

The Cessna 185 Skywagon is a six-seat, single-engine, general aviation light aircraft manufactured by Cessna. It made its first prototype flight in July 1960 and went into production in March 1961. Although more than 4,400 were built, production ceased in 1985. It is twenty-five feet and nine inches long with a wingspan of thirty-five feet and ten inches. The cruising speed in 145 knots. It is smaller, nimbler, and faster than the de Havillands. Later I flew in the Cessna 185 into the Congo. It's a delightful airplane.

Cessna 185

Chapter 9

Daily Journal

People who keep journals have life twice.
—Jessamyn West

I habitually keep a daily journal of all my adventuresome hiking, mountaineering, and canoeing experiences. They overflow my file cabinet. One of my most difficult tasks was to keep a detailed daily journal to document the entire canoe odyssey. By the end of the day, I was tired like the other voyageurs, but I was determined to keep track of everything that was significant. I tried to document how far we traveled and what the water and weather conditions were. I wrote every evening by my candle lantern while being serenaded by the other five paddlers blissfully snoring into the night.

JOHN KUDLAS

First Water

July 10, 1983

This is the day we have been planning for months…to fly in, splash down, and begin to run the Hayes. We were anxious to pull and push water under the canoes. It turned out to be a delightful fun- and work-filled day. The day seemed benevolent with the warm sun bathing our faces and calm water on the lake beneath the docked airplanes poised to take us aloft. Even the fish were glad to see us, biting everything we threw while we waited. The mosquitos were also happy to see us.

George, our baseball-fan pilot, and Tony, the other stoic pilot, directed us to strap two of the canoes on the pontoon assembly of the de Havilland Otter, the larger aircraft, into which Denny, Bill, and I loaded packs and seated, securing our seatbelts. Tony was our assertive pilot, and we were all ready.

George flew Mike and Lee in the smaller Cessna, depositing them on a small island first, then returned to the base to fetch Steve and the rest of the gear in a de Havilland Beaver, a plane larger than the Cessna but smaller than the Otter.

We finally left for Molson Lake at about 1:30 p.m. George and Tony flipped the starters, and the planes roared to life. We taxied to the larger area of the lake and roared even louder to gain flight speed until we were sent aloft. I sat in the copilot seat of the Otter with the headphones on so I could hear the two pilots communicate. During the flight, George circled the Cessna around the Otter to check our canoe load, which produced substantial parasite air drag, slowing us down a bit. He reported that everything was okay, so we continued. From the air, one could see how vast and rich Canada really is—a beautiful country with endless forests and nameless lakes. Tony was quiet but interesting. We had several horseflies gathered on the windshield. The Canadians call them bulldogs, and we found out later why they were called bulldogs by how they would bite. Instead of squashing and killing the nasty insects, Tony would gently grab each one by a wing, crank his window down slightly, and release it unharmed to freedom. I was impressed.

The Cessna circling us to check our load of canoes

Just before landing, I could see where the Hayes exited Molson Lake, so I knew the starting point and took a bearing with my compass. We landed smoothly, taxied to a small island, and gathered our canoes, equipment, and thoughts. Lee cast the first spoon and collected the first fish, a small Jack (northern pike). We kept very few fish on the trip, only when we needed one to eat. It was emotional watching the planes taxi back out to the middle of the lake and leave, knowing we would have no communication with the outside world for several weeks. We were now on our own. We left the island at about 1:30 p.m., pulling on our paddles with hopeful anticipation.

The de Havilland Otter leaving us…alone

We disembarked with a "discussion." One voyager insisted on going in a different direction. I try to always know where I am and where I need to go. Besides, I saw the start of the Hayes from the plane and took a bearing. So I continued the correct heading that I had calibrated from the plane. Arguing is usually counterproductive, and I found the best policy is to allow people to make mistakes to learn if safety is not a factor. Soon the two other canoes were following Steve and me. There were no further directional discussions.

We discovered that the Canadian topo maps and our impressions of river structure/barriers did not coincide with our USA topo maps. What they considered riffles, we would call rapids; what we would consider falls, they would consider rapids; and what they considered falls were portages for us. We learned to adjust our thinking. Water vocalization was the most accurate indicator. Roaring water was always concerning.

The first third and fourth rapids were just large riffles. The second one proved to be a beautiful waterfall, and at the base of the cascading water was a large congregation of northerns (Jacks), most in the four-to-five-pound range. We delighted in catching and releasing many of the Jacks before continuing our voyage. We had to remind ourselves that this was not a fishing trip and disciplined ourselves to limit our casting.

We decided to camp on islands as often as possible to provide a water barrier to bears or other foraging creatures that might disturb our slumber. And hopefully, the island would be open enough to allow a breeze to impede mosquitos. We found an inviting island at 10:00 p.m., but there was still some daylight. The mosquitoes were still quite bad because there was no breeze, so we quickly donned our head nets, found three tent sites, and erected our abodes. Mike soon had the pots chattering on the fire, and we had a late dinner. We were quite tired and crawled into our sleeping bags at midnight. This was our first night camping by the river. We were tired but joyous and spunky.

I was quite anguished when I soaked my mechanical "wind-up" pocket watch while running the rapids. I cherished the watch because I carefully glued a picture of Donna, my wife, and Josie, my faithful springer spaniel, inside the "snap-open" lid. I spent much of the evening blowing water out of the mechanism and holding it close to the fire, attempting to dry out the device. The watch came back to life with a resounding *tick*, and my lovely girls were saved. I then secured the cherished timing device into my waterproof camera box for safekeeping and only checked the time to run sections of the river, to sail lakes, and reclaim memories from the pictures. I would wind it and smile at my girls every evening before retiring for the rest of the trip.

My cherished watch with Donna and Josie's picture.
I used to time lake and rapids runs.

We proclaimed the island "mad bird island" because I was viciously attacked by a small unidentifiable songbird while scouting the island campsite. It struck me twice in the chest to my horror and surprise. Other voyagers laughed with delight at my plight. The bird probably had a nest nearby and was defending its home range. During the entire trip, we observed, to our delight, wildlife that we were anxious to see. Many ducks, mostly mergansers, decoyed us by feigning injury and paddling away from their clutch of youngsters, who quickly swam into the bulrushes. They swam like portable eggbeaters churning across the water. We also saw several bald eagles that graced the sky, seemingly welcoming us, and a bull moose with its antlers still in velvet who materialized in the bend of the river. We got some great pictures, but the moose soon became bored with posing and dissolved into the alders. We found three semilevel sites, brushed the debris from the site, erected our tents, and rolled out our sleeping pads and bags. Food was stowed under the canoes because there were no trees to hang the food packs. Soon we were nocturnally serenading the wilderness.

Preparing to shove off after our first night in the wilderness. Rain often greeted us.

Typical island campsite

In wooded campsite. Notice ice scars on tree from the spring's ice flow

The Long Portage

July 11, 1983

    The morning was a surprise. Rain started during the early morning and threatened to sink the island. It was the type of rain that Noah must have experienced. We knew we would be cast upon rough waters with sheets of rain filling our hats, clothes, and canoes. This was our first test of how we would cope with the elements and insect tormentors! Even though the night was windy and wet, we escaped the island by noon, paddling hard to dodge rain drops—an unsuccessful venture.

    In the hard rain, Steve and I missed the first portage! We heard the thundering water crashing below, so we turned back before being vacuumed down the churning rocks. We coasted across the upper edge of the cascade and looked down the chaos of crashing water, knowing we could not run the rapids with the loaded canoes. We knew there must be a portage, so we began searching in panicked earnest. After some searching, we finally found an old portage with blazed marks on the trees. We shored and secured the canoes, tramping through the forest for an hour in the ever-increasing deluge while following the blaze marks to an old tramway. The tramway was used in the distant past to haul the large York boats loaded with furs destined for Hudson Bay and ultimately to Europe. Some of the telltale rails were still in place with decomposed ties still loosely attached and a set of antiquated iron wheels, all being reclaimed by nature. They now stood silently and lonely among engulfing vegetation, looking terribly out of place like a giant set of barbells left by some awesome voyageur weightlifter of the past. I was tempted to lift them, but there was nobody to impress my lifting prowess with except the stoic, dripping cedars. Perhaps they were weeping with laughter at this puny wilderness Olympian.

We scampered back up the trail and discovered that Steve and I had narrowly missed the portage earlier. We had devised whistle signals, and I blew my whistle violently to turn the other canoes back away from the falls. Suddenly I could see them returning. They were puzzled and worried about where we were. After some sheepish explaining, we were now ready to begin the arduous task of portaging canoes and gear.

Portaging the equipment and canoes

We hauled all the equipment and supplies down the long portage in the rain. I would guess it was about three-quarters of a mile long to the base of the falls where we could paddle again. The portage was wide (for the York boats) and relatively smooth but very wet. It was raining so hard that the trail became a stream. I had trout fished in smaller streams back home. The water was up to my knees and looked like chocolate milk. Occasionally I would step into a hole and stumble about, trying not to fall facedown into the quagmire while fully loaded and lose the load in the swirling stream.

We finally transported everything down to the base of the falls where I looked the troops over. They were a sorry-looking soaked bunch, and it would have been humorous had we not been so miserable. We just sat on our canoes for a while, gasping and looking at each other. But nobody despaired or said anything negative—a good sign.

Bill dug out some food and prepared lunch for the hungry marauders. And suddenly the sun graciously exposed itself, peeking through the towering trees! The combination of food and sunlight ignited our spirits, and we were soon jostling about again, laughing off the experience.

We did not fish because we lost about two hours on the portage. I felt bad that I did not take any pictures of the artifacts we found but didn't want to open my camera box in the downpour. I especially wanted to get a photo of an interesting tree observed. It had been tapped years ago for its pitch to seal canoes and York boats of yesteryear. It was obvious that it had healed over only to be re-punctured again several times over—living proof of bygone voyageurs.

We cast off in dripping wet clothes, heading downriver to our next campsite: an inviting boreal paradise. Mike soon had the pots vibrating with wholesome food. After a short discussion, we retired without fanfare, just listening to humming mosquitos.

Sailing the Hayes

July 12, 1983

I arose at 5:00 a.m. to a glowing, promising day! It was as delightful and gracious as yesterday was awful and threatening. Yesterday was wet and cold, and today was warm and dry—quite a contrast. It did not seem like the same place.

We started the day early, as the group had agreed, to try and make up lost time in the storm. Moisture had permeated everything, and everything was still wet and soggy. And the mosquitos had fed on Steve and me all night because in my haste, I had misaligned the tent closure before retiring, and the bloodthirsty critters climbed in at will. The tent was no longer a sleeping abode but a sacrificial altar! And a smelly one at that. The sweaty voyageurs in wet wool clothing made for a gamy environment. I was afraid the tents were going to smell like locker rooms!

The day became more gorgeous as we paddled in the placid azure river. We began taking off clothing, and soon we were all joyously paddling in our undershorts. Then the rapids began, and we needed to regain a serious attitude and poise for action. We regained our composure and reassembled our wardrobe to face the noisy challenge. We ran the first large rapids with empty canoes and portaged the gear. Then we confidently ran the rest of the rapids fully packed and loaded until the last one that we portaged around before entering Opi (Opiminegoka) Lake. The lake opened to us like a stage with us as actors entering for the first act. Now we felt like true voyageurs matching wits and skills with the boiling rapids like old paddlers. But we knew there were more challenging adventures waiting ahead!

During the planning stage of the excursion, we discovered that Bill Mason, a well-known author of canoeing books, wrote about making a sailboat out of two or three canoes. We thought this might be a good idea for traversing some of the large lakes to save our hands from cranking the paddles in the rapids. So we decided to lash our boats together into a sailing vessel to cross Opi Lake. We lashed three canoes side by side with the middle canoe slightly ahead of the others and the aft portion of the ship slightly wider in a fantail configuration so water would not pile up between the canoes. Slender birch limbs were crossed over the three canoes and lashed to the thwarts with bungee cords. The "mast" was two other light birch logs attached to the front thwarts of the outside canoes and cross-erected vertically. The mast was hoisted aloft with a heroic attitude and a line attached to it and the bow and stern of the middle canoe. We carried a large nylon sheet to use as the sail and for a rainfly as needed. The middle of the sheet was then attached to the mast, and lines were attached to the sheet corners and secured by the grommets in the sheet. The sail was held by the "captain" of the ship to control the wind attack. Two outside-canoe sternmen controlled the boat's direction with their paddles, acting as rudders at the bequest of the captain. While the ship was being rigged, Bill fixed lunch, which we voraciously inhaled.

We were still wet and decided to take advantage of the blessed sun before sailing. We each took turns swimming and taking a "bath" to the delight of each tent partner. All the equipment and clothes were hung out on tree branches or draped over bushes to dry while we frolicked in the water. The island stop was breezy, which enhanced drying and shooed off insect invaders. It was a rewarding respite.

But we were anxious to sail! We quickly repacked, reloaded, and took a compass bearing from the map to the river outlet, and were soon sailing high seas of Opi Lake like voyageurs in their York boats. Steve and Denny employed the tacking lines while Mike and I controlled the rudders. Lee struggled to try and dry out his camera in the sun, and Bill played big-game fisherman, trolling for sailfish. The improvised craft performed flawlessly, grasping the wind and slicing the three canoes through the pristine waters of the huge lake as designed.

Because music is the vital mental tonic, we were soon telling stories and singing "Gilligan's Island." We were joyously flying through liquid sky!

> Just sit right back, and you'll hear a tale,
> A tale of a fateful trip
> That started from this tropic port
> Aboard this tiny ship.
> The mate was a mighty sailing man,
> The skipper brave and sure.
> Five passengers set sail that day
> For a three-hour tour, a three-hour tour.
>
> The weather started getting rough,
> The tiny ship was tossed,

If not for the courage of the fearless crew
The Minnow would be lost, the Minnow would
 be lost.

The ship set ground on the shore of this uncharted
 desert isle
With Gilligan
The Skipper too,
A millionaire and his wife,
A movie star
The Professor and Mary Ann,
Here on Gilligan's Isle. (www.lyricsondemand.com)

Tacking the wind with our marvelous sailing ship

    Everything had been going so well. We were on an emotional high, like winning an important competitive team event, so we wanted to rest and relax for a while after such a rewarding day. We returned to shore at 6:00 p.m. on an island near the mouth of the Hayes River. It was a perfect spot with wind to keep the insects at bay, wood for the fire, level areas for our three tents, and a luxurious view that money rarely could buy. This campsite is etched in our memories, and we knew it would be difficult to leave come morning. We each went to a lonely place on the island for our quiet time to reflect on what we have done and the challenges ahead—a time for meditation. Then we were treated to one of Mike's delicious compositions.

We surrendered to our tents and retired to our inviting sleeping bags to the rasping sound of a distant raven gargling, lofted in a dead tree across the bay. If only the rest of the voyage could be this pleasant. We knew better.

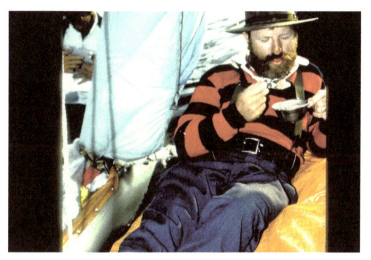

Tacking the sail with my toes while having breakfast.
Note Bill's sleeping bag drying on the aft line.

Windy Lake Hordes

July 13, 1983

It was a windy day of sailing rough "seas" and a great day for running the whitewaters of the Hayes.

I awoke as usual at 5:00 a.m. to a humming-drumming sound interrupted by an occasional flopping-popping sound. Curious, I rolled on my side and was astonished as what I witnessed. The rising sun cast a shadow image through the tent fabric, which acted as a theater screen and percussion instrument. There were so many mosquitos between my tent and the rainfly that they made a rhythmic, melodious humming sound; and the interrupting sound, like a bass drum, was a large toad clumsily leaping onto my tent, gathering morsels of mosquitos for breakfast. It was entertaining but worrisome because I knew I would have to go out into the bloodthirsty hordes to fend for myself. I studied the toad and cheered him on until I looked at my zippered screen. I could barely make out the outdoor environment through the mass of mosquitos that had found us during the night. They were lying in wait, knowing we would have to emerge from the tent. But it had to be done.

Mosquitos and coffee awaited us every morning.

I quickly put on all my clothes, gloves, and head net. I warned Steve to cover his head and prepared to exit the tent. I inhaled deeply like I was going to jump out of an airplane, unzipped the screen, and dove out into the cloud of thirsty insects. I then turned and rezippered the tent as quickly as I could. I had prepared tinder and kindling for the fire the night before and soon had a snapping fire, and I added green pine boughs occasionally for smoke to ward off airborne invaders. Soon Mike joined me and made coffee (always the first thing) and created a great breakfast. We rousted up the other paddlers, and everyone scurried to eat and break camp. We did not want to tarry long.

Early morning embarkment to escape mosquitos. Note the head nets.

We shored the "sailboat" on the lee side of the island the night before but wisely kept it erected for a hasty escape. We thought we could make the ship more effective and maneuverable by adding an upper boom to display the sail wider. Soon we were cutting water down the wide river again.

We joyfully sailed down the river and Windy Lake with a carefree attitude, chatting, joking as usual, and basking in the delightful sun. We expected the weather to be cold, but the air temperature was quite pleasant; it was in the seventies and lower eighties. The voyage to and across the lake was tricky due to strong wind that broke the improvised upper boom with a resounding *snap* about halfway across the lake. We stopped and replaced the upper boom and decided to add a lower boom to capture even more wind. We also attached lines to the ends of each boom for added control and to tack sideways to the wind more effectively, and we added an improvised keel for stability. My, were we clever! And an efficient crew now with Denny in charge of the keel; Mike, Lee, and Bill manning the rudders and occasionally paddling; and me handling the lines and controlling sail attitude to capture the wind. We laughed that we had passed through a couple of hundred years of sail evolutionary developments in a few hours.

At the end of the lake, we released the booms and mast and paddled down the narrower portion of the Hayes again, dancing among the boulders, canoes spaced apart for safety, and with the essential cook kit coming in the last canoe. It was always good to see the cook kit and food packs come down the rapids safely. We were challenged by three good rapids to Robinson Falls, and all the rapids fell prey to our canoeing prowess as we flew down the rapids with great skill. We were getting cocky, which is a dangerous phenomenon.

At the base of the falls, we all withdrew our fishing weapons and lashed at the waters. We all caught large northern pike, but Denny championed the largest at thirty-five inches and, we figured, over eight pounds. Interestingly, Denny confessed that this was the first fish he had ever caught! What fun to see the joy on his face as he giggled and slapped his knee!

We camped on a small island at the entrance to Oxford Lake and dined on northern pike fillets and other delicacies prepared by Mike. It was a meal any president would have enjoyed. We decided to retire early and sleep late to prepare the sailboat for the long trek across the large freshwater flashing sea—Oxford Lake.

I could see the moon through the screened tent door and recalled the pact Donna, my wife, and I made: that we both would look at the moon every night at 10:00 p.m. and think of each other. I opened my pocket watch, looked at her lovely picture, and said, "I love you," and, "Good night." Then I snapped the lid shut. I slept clutching the precious watch.

Oxford Lake Monster

July 14, 1983

Upon awakening and charging from my tent, I discovered we had been attacked by a monster during the night! Well, sort of a monster attack. This is what happened:

Mike mixed a batch of sourdough the night before and set the filled pans on a nearby boulder to rise during the night. The dough had risen and overflowed the pans and engulfed the packs, equipment, and rocky platform. The dough had grown to enormous proportions, and like a giant amoeba, it grasped everything nearby. I began chuckling at the sight and soon was belly laughing. The other voyagers quickly arose and joined in with their own festive analysis. We sat there for some time until we realized the mess would have to be cleaned up. Mercifully, Denny tactfully addressed the chore by scooping up the critter and saving the mess to be made into pancakes and baked over the fire for lunch bread. That was about 8:00 a.m. There was a slight breeze that kept the insects away, and a nice sunlit day greeted our spirits and encouraged us to continue in earnest. We were eager to continue our quest.

After another great breakfast, minus the anticipated sourdough pancakes, we set out to build a new sailboat. Lee and I hastily cut and erected the masts and sail while Denny and Mike worked on the thwart connectors. We made the vessel extra sturdy because we were going to sail the mighty Oxford Lake. But we were in for a disappointing surprise.

There was hardly any wind, and it was like we were in the equatorial doldrums. With the sailboat intact, we paddled the best we could down the end of the river to the giant lake. At the entrance of the lake, we stopped and had one of Bill's great lunches of bannock, cheese, and hard salami. The sea was vast and ominously silent, so we proceeded to cross the lake via people power. Denny, Lee, Bill, and Steve paddled the sailboat through the dead water while Mike manned the rudder and I held the tact lines, praying for a latent breeze to spell our arms.

The sourdough dough that attacked us during the night

The lake seemed peaceful and serene, but the lake had its own plan. She was not going to allow a flimsy craft improvised from three rigged canoes to spoil her reputation! She grew angry and spat upon us—innocent, novice voyagers. The sudden wind in our faces was now the enemy! We retreated to a small cove on the lee side of a small, lonely island for protection from the gusting wind. We hastily struggled to made camp in the tortuous wind lashing at our flimsy abodes. The tents and rainflies flapped in the gale, acting more like warning flags.

While we paddled the silent water during the day, we had glorious ideas about ghost sailing all night via compass, stars, and the moon; but Oxford Lake humbled us back to human reality and safety. We retired about 10:45 p.m., exhausted but satisfied that we were safe, listening to the crashing waves licking tongues of foaming whitewater across our boulders and sailboat. The thundering wind and waves made it difficult to sleep, but we finally accepted the sound as an ominous lullaby.

I lay there, writing in my journal. *What would tomorrow bring?* I wondered as I tried to slumber, clutching my pocket watch.

Marooned on Oxford Lake

July 15, 1983

Yes, we were marooned like a pirate shipwreck on a desolate island!

Nevertheless, the island was a great refuge. There was a safe cove for our tethered ship, soft level tent sites, and few nasty mosquitos, deerflies, and bulldogs. We took great delight in watching the dragonflies catch and devour the nasty intruders. One dragonfly landed on Mike's finger and munched a deer fly, to our cheers and applause! The dragonflies patrolled our camp out of the wind like allied helicopters on a search and destroy mission. I thought we should name this island in their honor: Dragonfly Island.

I got up at 5:00 a.m. to the clatter of our noble vessel's delicate hull butting against the rocky shore of the tiny island of refuge. The wind was blowing like a thousand banshees, threatening to release our boat and rip our tents to shreds. I crawled out of the tent, trying to stay low and stealthily snaking down to our little bay to secured the craft more tightly with the lines to the shoreline trees. I then crawled back into my sleeping bag nested in the flapping tent. I arose again at 8:00 a.m. and looked around with disgust at the rainstorm in a spate of annoyance and again at 10:00 a.m. to assess the seething wind strength and possible damage. It was not encouraging. I knew we would be there awhile, captive. The whitecaps were high, and the wind still in our faces. I couldn't help thinking of Wordie's words, "It's an ill wind that does nobody good." In the *Endurance*, a crew member of that ship sank while attempting to reach Antarctica.

Oxford Lake storm threatening us again

The sailboat moored out of the wind but
ready in a small cove on the island

Suddenly the rest of crew materialized: first Denny, then Mike, then Bill, then Lee, and finally Steve. All were amazed at the turbid waters and the power of nature around us. We felt like feeble creatures, humbled and diminutive at the mercy of nature's wrath. But we took a philosophic resigned attitude to make the best of the situation.

The rest of the day continued to be very windy and then became hot, so we all took a bath in our little private bay and washed the perspiration from our steamy clothes. Mike kept us entertained with good food like cake, bannock, and spaghetti, the scents of wafted throughoutout the campsite. Of course, everyone had yarns to tell, and we all retreated to our tents or an inviting boulder to spend some time reading. I started reading Sig Olson's *Lonely Land* again while peeking out of my tent often to watch the sky, looking for a message of hope. But the clouds would not allow the sky to show through.

In the late evening, I got up and sat upon a granite boulder on the island's northern point and anxiously watched as sheets of storm flowed across the vast lake like somebody had spilled black ink across the sky. Shafts of lighting glowed across the dark *nimbostratus* clouds in the sky and struck nearby points while thunder rumbled around us, like *Thor* wielding his hammer and *Zeus* hurling thunderbolts. The power of the storm was awesome and offered surreal incongruity between our plight and the serene beauty of the black clouds. Although we were an unflinching, tight, loyal unit, it was getting difficult to hold members of the crew intact. We were already two days behind schedule, and mutiny seemed possible. All members of the crew were anxious to continue. Minds urged our muscle and sinew to continue.

We made the decision to wait until 3:00 a.m. tomorrow morning before moving on regardless of the weather. The evening air was turning cold, so I was hoping for a calming effect upon the weather and the crew. I was mostly concerned about getting swamped by the towering whitecaps if we continued in haste into the jaws of the storm.

We readied the equipment and retired early for an early start in the morning. My ears were tuned to quietness, but the wind continued to howl—a threatening reminder of lurking disaster.

A Day of Toil, Disappointment, and Joy

July 16, 1983

The relentless storm with its fierce beauty continued, and we were incarcerated in our flimsy, flapping tents, trying to wait out the deluge to no avail. I crawled out of our tent to inspect our boat at 11:30 p.m. the night before and at 3:30 a.m. and 4:30 a.m., hoping to announce good news, but nature's wrath was still descending on us. Bill continued to quarry, "What do you think?" Finally, we decided to try to make it across Oxford Lake, about sixteen to eighteen miles, to Oxford House—a Cree village that was once a Hudson Bay outpost. We noisily dismantled our tents in a frenzy, secured everything in the bottom of the bobbing ship bowels, and covered all the secured equipment with the spray skirts to prevent loss before shoving off, paddling hard in synchrony on the sides with the sail wrapped/reefed and stowed away. We hopped from island to island, resting briefly behind each island to catch our breath and rest our arms and backs, which were numb with fatigue. We watched in horror as the inky cloud vortex would circle the lake and repeatedly slash our faces and douse us with sheets of rain, howling wind, and crashing whitecaps. We watched as the black phenomenon circled, stalking us. We felt like prey.

Approaching Oxford House through the whistling wind

The whitecaps would spill over our spray skirts and splash into the canoe's bowels, threatening to soak clothes and gear. We had to continually bail the water out with sponges and cooking pots to stay afloat. Whoever was not paddling was bailing. We initially laced the bottom of our canoes with alder branches. But they only added to the mess, so we discontinued the practice. It was a hard pull. We were quite exhausted, and our arms ached.

We finally caught sight of some fishing boats shored up beside some small unkept houses. It was Oxford House! We made it! We erroneously thought we outpaddled the storm and won the struggle to the mouth of the Hayes River. Suddenly the Cree inhabitants of the houses came out to greet us. We really felt welcomed, and it was exciting, almost like a homecoming celebration. The children looked with wonderment, and most of the adults giggled and laughed at our flimsy sailboat and questioned our flag. The Rochester (out host city) flag always proudly flew from the mast of our ship, but the Crees wondered what country we were from. We tried to explain Rochester and Minnesota, but they did not understand. We asked one man stoically watching from shore where the Hudson Bay store was. But since he could not understand English, he sent one of the children to fetch his wife. She came dashing out of the house while wrapping herself in a tattered sweater, giggling down to the shore, excited to have visitors. She was about thirty years old and could not communicate well either because she lacked teeth. We really wanted to get to the Hudson Bay store because we knew we could radio home and tell our families we were okay. We knew they would be worrying.

After unsuccessfully trying to get information from the lady, I simply yelled, "Hudson Bay store." She nodded affirmatively and pointed down the rocky shore. I held up my fingers to get an idea how far it was, and she held up two fingers. Then I asked what the store color was by tapping on the boat they had on shore and shouting, "Red." She nodded again and said, "Yellow." We thanked her, bid goodbye to our new friends, and paddled on. Apparently, she did not understand English as well as her husband thought because the Hudson Bay store was about five miles around the bend and was grey with a signature red roof. Just before reaching the store, the storm returned to soak us again and nearly filled our canoes. Ugh!

Cree family greeting us and giving us directions

Suddenly the abated storm moved on to torture others, and the blessed sun came out. I remember looking at the paddlers and seeing the glow of the sun on their faces and in their spirits. We took turns going into the store, which was like Walmart to the Cree because you could buy just about anything there. Steve did not have a wife to call, so he guarded the boat and tried to answer questions from the inquisitive youngsters with busy hands. We became quite concerned with all the young giggling girls that found Steve attractive, but Steve handled the situation well with his glowing eyes, baritone chuckle, and ivory teeth.

It was finally my turn to call home, and I choked up upon hearing Myke's (our twelve-year-old son) voice. He asked, "Dad, is that really you?" almost like he thought he would never hear from me again. I did not realize how much I missed him, Kari (our thirteen-year-old daughter), Josie (my faithful springer), and of course, my sweet Donna. I found it difficult chatting, but I eventually collected myself and informed them that we were safe and glad to hear that they were safe. For the first time, I was anxious to complete the voyage and be with my family. But we had a ways to go yet. We were not yet even halfway.

Before leaving the store, I purchased an English taffy bar as a treat. It was hard as granite, but it lasted a long time. As I pushed the door open to exit the store, I saw an ominous caution notice on bulletin board stating that the water in the huge lake was not fit to drink! The note was written in the Cree cuneiform-style script and in English. Of course, we had been drinking water from the river the entire trip, and we had no filter system to implement. Ironically, we found that palatable, safe water was a difficult commodity to procure for the rest of the trip. Giardia had infected some of the water, and besides, the lower end of the river became quite cloudy and euphoric.

We quickly threw in the few things we purchased, distributed family news among the paddlers, and shoved off. Upon entering the Hayes River again, we released the cross thwarts and mast to the beavers and paddled placid waters to Back Lake. We selected a site on an island at about 8:30 p.m. We had crackers and peanut butter, we set up camp, and we retired early. Tomorrow we would start running rapids again, and then move on to Knee Lake—another large body of water with many threatening false bays to get lost in. Navigation would be critical. We slumbered peacefully with little communication, hoping and praying for a favorable wind so we can sail the lake to save time and energy. Steve and I studied the map to implant the route in our minds.

Whitewater Problems and Piscatorial Prizes

July 17, 1983

I will always remember this day as the day when we laughed at the whitewater challenges and when the whitewater angrily sneered back. I will also remember it as a day when, for the first time, I could have caught all the walleyes I desired to land!

We got up at 5:30 a.m., gulped a quick breakfast, broke camp, and were soon cascading across Back Lake. Then we exited the lake, went back into the Hayes, and ran all the rapids with resolve toward Knee Lake. We stopped at Trout Falls for a lunch break, for repairs, and to prepare our sailboat below the falls to sail the ever-widening river. We all had problems in Knife Rapids. And we now understood why it was named Knife Rapids. Slatelike rocks stood on end like sinister knife blades or shark teeth, daring us to ingloriously attempt to run our canoes through their jaws. But we were undaunted and didn't shirk or hesitate as we slid down the gullet of the rapids.

Disaster… The rapids won! Steve and I sheered a couple of rivets off the bottom of our canoe and bent the keel on a "blocker" rock. Lee and Mike loosened some rivets on their keel, which produced a substantial leak. And Denny and Bill were pinned against some boulders and swamped. They finally wisely jumped into the rapids and released the horrific stream power, correctly pointing their canoe downstream. They wisely held on to the stern on opposite sides and glided downstream safely, feet first, to an eddy where we could help them empty and reenter their canoe and continue downstream.

So when we stopped at Trout Falls, it was time for needed repairs. Denny soon had his trusty tools out and was repairing the disabled vessels. His and Bill's canoe had the most damage with a long slice on its side, like a can opener did its business on it. Denny brought along some aluminum sheet stock and soon had a piece cut to fit, and he proceeded to drill holes through it and the canoe with a hand drill.

He riveted the patch in place, forming a tight, waterproof seal. Duct tape took care of the rest of the repairs, enough for us to complete the voyage anyway. Then everyone scattered their clothing over tree branches and bushes for the sun to dry them out. We all lay out in the basking sun with the dragonflies ever gleaning mosquitos off us. We learned not to swat the friendly Odonata, even when they landed on our faces. Some of us snoozed, oblivious of what was ahead.

Dennis repair-riveting a canoe patch

While waiting for the sun to do its magic and after gulping down lunch, I decided to trek down to the base of the falls. I gazed into the base of the falls and was surprised as to what was lounging at its base. Large golden fish were lurking in the rapids side by side. I was disgruntled at first because I thought they were large carp, which I did not expect to see. Then I realized they were trophy-sized walleyes! I quickly ran back up the portage trail beside the falls and got my spinning rod and reel out of my canoe, stumbling in my excitement. After returning to the base of the falls, the first cast yielded one of the monsters. I dashed back up to the lunch site and proudly held up the golden prize for the voyagers to admire. Soon we were all back below the falls. We each kept one for dinner and returned the others to their water sanctuary. They were wonderful to catch and delicious to eat!

We decided that we had fished enough and absorbed enough of the gracious sun, and it was time to reconstruct the sailboat below the falls and sail down the wide Hayes as far as we could. Steve and I carried the masts through the rapids while Lee and Mike followed with the sail and booms, then came Denny and Bill with the cross beams-thwarts. This was a poor idea because the increased load disturbed the balance in the canoes and made it difficult to maneuver in the rapids. Our effort to save a few birch limbs put us in jeopardy. We did not attempt this again.

We became efficient shipbuilders, and the vessel was prepared quickly. But much excitement occurred below the falls when we tried to cast off! The back current was sucking everything back under the falls and grabbed our precious boat from our grasp, threatening to destroy it. The falls would have smashed our boat and equipment to shreds and kept it underwater, lost forever. I quickly decided to jump into the water among the walleyes to secure the boat. The water was armpit-deep, and I was soaked. One of the lads tossed me a rope, and the crew hauled me and the boat to safety. My compass and binoculars were full of water, to my dismay, but everything else was dry and safe.

We were excited because the sun was out and the wind was at our backs—an inviting scenario. We could sail down much of the large river to save our strength. We sailed about twenty-five miles into Knee Lake, which we knew would be a difficult lake to navigate because there were many islands, false bays, and land points to confound bearings. This turned out to be problematic the next day. We had dreams of sailing during the night and consequently had dinner in the canoes, compliments of Denny's camp stove. He prepared a spartan meal in the stern of his canoe and passed food to hungry seamen. The dream dissolved at about 10:30 p.m. when we came upon an old Cree fishing camp. We erected our tents on dry wooden platforms that were designed to hold crates of whitefish for shipment. Darkness and fatigue prevailed, and we were soon slumbering again to the drumming of mosquitos outside our tents, threatening to invade.

More Sailing and Island Respite

July 18, 1983

Part of the day was glorious in terms of weather and wind while other parts of the day were hard paddling and paddle bracing. We arose at 5:30 a.m. to the humming/drumming of the mosquitos outside our tents again. It became a morning necessitating full body armor and head nets—an annoying morning ritual. Despite sealing my Duluth pack, my equipment, especially my precious sleeping bag, became soaked when our canoe was breeched in the rapids. So I spent a damp, uncomfortable night trying to get some needed sleep. After tossing and turning, I ended up sleeping directly on my air mattress and covering myself with the clammy tarp/sail to stay warm the best I could. But morning brought joy when I saw the wind was in our favor to sail and the sun smiling at us!

A disagreement developed during breakfast. The two navigators, Steve and Lee, disagreed on where we were and which way we should go. I always tried to know where we were and what bearing to take. One of the navigators was correct, and the other was wrong but insisted he was correct. Not wanting to destroy the harmony of the group, I took over navigating across Knee Lake. Interestingly, the lake is shaped like a leg and knee, so it was easy to misnavigate. Soon our spirits were reinvigorated like a dedicated team, and although we had to do some backtracking, we were off sailing down the upper leg of Knee Lake.

Because of the directional wind change, it was now in our disfavor at the knee junction; so we stopped, rolled up the sail, had lunch, and proceeded to paddle in our troika ship like Hawaiians against the wind. I navigated in the front-middle cockpit, trying to ascertain the outlet of the Hayes, while other voyageurs paddled hard. Everyone preferred to paddle to stay occupied, warm, and useful. We skirted the myriad of islands for protection and to rest. Gorp and Kool-Aid were often passed among the loyal paddlers. We finally struggled our way to the lower leg of Knee Lake, and the wind was in our faces again. No sailing, just hard paddling. We retired the sail and wrapped it around one of the booms again, but the ship stayed intact for stability.

The wind changed direction, and we thought we could take advantage of nature's free force. We desperately set up our sail and tacked and paddled across the large part of the huge lake with all the deliberate speed we could muster. Islands were sparse, and we did not want to become stranded overnight on the open water. Suddenly we saw a large white structure in the distance. I squinted though my field glasses and thought it might be a float plane. Our spirits soured because we thought we might get some news. Any news from the outside world would have been great. But it was to no avail! It was a small island totally engulfed with white seagulls. We bid them goodbye and sailed on, disappointed.

Near dusk, we came upon a lonely, beautiful, picturesque island! It was high with a rocky shoreline and a soft interior mossy womb for our infant tents. We quickly staked our tents, facing them to the lovely sunset and breeze to delight our eyes and cool our faces. Another pleasant surprise was that the island was inhabited by a myriad of hungry spiders with latticed, webbed insect traps. We watched with glee as the efficient spiders caught the mosquitos that were stalking us. The spiders scurried across the network, killed their prey, and mummified/packaged them for later digestion. Oh, what joy!

We adopted several of the spiders and placed them inside our tents. They scurried to the apex and continued hunting the nasty mosquitos that snuck into our tent. The bloodthirsty insects would normally make for an uncomfortable night for us. With my hands behind my head as I lay in my sleeping bag, I silently applauded each capture. We retired at about 10:30 p.m., feeling we had a great day and praying for a favorable wind and good weather tomorrow. This was one of our favorite islands, Spider Island!

Our Spider Island haven

Our friends, the spiders, catching mosquitoes that were hunting us

Sweet Day That Turned Sour

July 19, 1983

The day began sweetly gentle but soured and curdled when we reached the rapids between Knee and Swampy Lakes. Then the day became bitterly miserable when we reached Swampy Lake, and we desperately tried to secure a campsite at midnight!

We arose about 7:00 a.m., had a hearty breakfast, took our usual pictures, and departed our paradise arachnid island under full sail with clear skies and a vast twenty-mile sea ahead of us. We read, wrote in our journals, and sunbathed while Mother Nature filled our sails, benevolently pushing us northeast. I handled the sail and map and compass while others took turns manning the rudder and tended their personal gear. It was placid, and we exchanged positive feelings about the trip and what we had accomplished so far, not knowing what was ahead. Things would change.

When we reached the end of the lake by late afternoon, I became concerned by the high water and remembered what the Mountie said at the onset of the voyage—that "the water was remarkably high." It looked like it was about two feet higher than normal. I could see and hear the hungry rapids waiting to devour fragile canoes. We dismantled the sailing craft, secured our loads, and prepared for potential disaster.

My suspicions were confirmed! The water was high and fast, and the rapids were violent and unpredictable. Steve and I ran the first rapids but signaled the other two canoes to portage the other canoes and equipment down the high and dry portage trail. Steve and I got dangerously cocky and decided to run the second rapids, which was a poor calculation. The standing waves were above our heads, and we went down the middle shoot with water swamping into our canoe. We dropped to our knees, and I remember shouting to Steve, "Keep straight!" The water was so swift and powerful that it grabbed our canoe like a toy and cast us down the rapids without concern. To turn and cascade sideways down the rapids would have been tragic, wiping us out on the boulders. I witnessed the bow of the canoe and Steve disappear into the watery abyss with the water slamming closed behind him like the final chapter of a scary book. Even though we paddled hard and straight downstream, we felt we were in a watery Armageddon, and we now needed to paddle hard to break out of the towering "keeper wave" that was trying to keep us in the rapids, pulling us back and under. We paddled through the clutching falls to an eddy purgatory at the end of the rapids and the portage, welcomed by our fellow paddlers who had wisely portaged after seeing our plight. We tried to bail out as much of the Hayes River out of our canoe as we could. Our canoe was almost entirely full of water. Our packs and canoe floatation kept us from totally submerging. But now everything was soaked!

And now nightfall was threatening, compounding the difficulties, but we had to continue down the river because the invading water had claimed any campsite that might have been promising along the river. We ended up running rapids under the illuminating full moon. All Steve and I could see was the wet labyrinth of rocks and boulders ahead of us and the glow of the aluminum canoes behind us. Steve and I led but instructed the other canoes to follow unless we swamped, then they should find an alternative route, perhaps through the partially submerged cedars inhabiting the shores, to escape. Going down the rapids was especially concerning because all I could see ahead in the moonlight was the dancing water, bald wet boulders, and towering trees. I knew we would be dropping down precipitously because all we could see were sentinel conifer treetops along the river, warning us that we would be dropping down quickly. We paddled and struggled on through to a quiet sanctuary, expecting to see Swampy Lake, only to be greeted by yet another treacherous rapids. This section of the river was a litany of water horror, especially at night.

We finally made it to Swampy Lake at about 11:30 p.m., but there were still no dry campsites to greet us! We paddled by the drowning tree-studded shoreline, desperately seeking dry salvation, but none could be found. Suddenly Lee found a large beaver lodge that was domed with chaotic sticks and logs. But it was dry, so we stopped for a respite to catch our breath before continuing to the end of the dark lake. We dozed awhile under our sail/rainfly then reluctantly pushed on. We finally stopped at a small island that was infested with our ubiquitous unfriendly mosquitos. Steve and I set up our tent, took off our wet clothes, and prepared to spend a wet night in soggy sleeping bags. Denny and Bill graciously shared their sleeping bags, and they slept in dry clothes on their air mattresses. All of Steve's and some of my equipment and clothes were soaked. We retired at about 1:00 a.m., soggy, hungry, exhausted, and somewhat discouraged. I now know why this body of water was named Swampy Lake. We dozed off anyway, too tired to be miserable.

A Day of Anticipation

July 20, 1983

This was a day of anticipation because we were approaching the point of no return. This is where the Hayes exits Swampy Lake, continues until it is joined with Gods River, and then continues on to Hudson Bay.

I got up at about 8:00 a.m. but did not know for sure what the time was because my wristwatch was waterlogged. I wisely stowed my pocket watch, compass, and camera in the waterproof aluminum box before being swallowed by the rapids. Steve had a lot of clothes to dry, and I had a few items that needed drying. Bill also wanted to inventory and reorganize the dwindling food packs, so we decided to have a work/organizational day before tackling the next worrisome rapids. After things had dried off and Bill was content with the food inventory, we finally disembarked the awful mosquito infested island at about 3:00 p.m., paddling our canoes in tandem in a single file until we reached a wilderness hunting camp where we stopped to have lunch prepared by Bill. Sadly, we found a dead bald eagle that looked like it had been shot.

We again lashed our canoes together because whitecaps were developing over the shallow lower end of Swampy Lake. We then paddled our raft together until we reached a small island at the end of the lake where the Hayes greeted us again. It was a beautiful island with high rocky tent platforms, wind to shoo the mosquitos away, and plenty of dead wood for fuel. We bathed in the surprisingly warm water and washed our clothes. We felt revived. Later in the evening, we had popcorn for a treat before retiring. I peeked at the picture of my loved ones in my pocket watch's lid before retiring to my glamorous sleeping bag at about 11:00 p.m. I slumbered while listening to the loons yodeling back and forth across the lake. It was a lullaby everyone should experience.

French Cuisine

July 21, 1983

We were on the move again, in more ways than one. Last night after writing in my journal, Mike, Denny, and I all got severe stomach cramps. I soon discovered the value of knowing where the spade and toilet paper were and to be careful of my suspenders while relieving myself in the cathole in the forest. We competed for the small shovel during this emergency event! We soon felt better, then we packed and ran the river again.

We ran several small percolating rapids and portaged around three others. We had to bushwhack around the largest rapids because we could not find the portage and could hear the threatening roar of the snarling rapids. Steve and I considered running the vocal rapids, but we learned our lesson and decided to haul the equipment through the forest. After viewing the rapids from our rocky, lofty position, it was obvious we made a wise decision and felt we would not have made the watery route without capsizing. Steve calculated that we progressed ten miles and have seventeen rapids and twelve more miles to go before the waters became less threatening and more peaceful.

Strangely, Steve and Mike encouraged us to fish for the colorful giant brook trout that were snapping mayfly invertebrates molting on the water's surface while they prepared dinner. It was a strange request because there is usually much to do around the bustling camp, but we joyfully obeyed. We caught and released several fish and returned to an amazing camp scene. Now we knew what Steve and Mike had been plotting!

Steve was an amateur magician and brought his tuxedo in his pack. He served us French-waiter style with a white dish towel draped over his arm and addressed us with his best French accent. He "seated" us (on our packs) individually as special guests with assigned positions. He served the meal designed and prepared by Mike, which included juice, salad, hors d'oeuvres, a main dish of beef jerky stew, apple dumpling for dessert, and an after-dinner toast. It was a special touching affair being formally served in French style in the middle of the Canadian wilderness. Inverted canoes were our formal tables. Three waterfalls encircling us acted as our orchestra playing our favorite bubbly melody—the music of moving rhythmic water. The stars twinkled overhead, and the moon rose as dusk fell upon us while a coral of melodious loons serenading us. What an experience! Our team seated and ate a special meal while Steve and Mike proudly stood, embracing our pleasure of a delicious meal. This was an unexplainable awesome experience.

Mike and Steve serving us the surprise French dinner

After thanking our hosts, we all retired early to get some needed rest for tomorrow's unknown adventuresome push. It was the earliest I had retired for some time—9:00 p.m., I thought as I meditated and opened my pocket watch to say good night to my loved ones. I sighed with contentment and joy.

Successful Rapids Running

July 22, 1983

I awoke at 5:30 a.m. to the sound of a threating thunderstorm rumbling along the forest canopy with flashes of ominous lightning. It moved upon us and engulfed us like a giant macroinvertebrate, threatening to digest us like microorganisms. In an act of cowardice, I stayed in my warm sleeping bag, ignoring the rain, shafts of radiance, and looming darkness until about 8:00 a.m. when I peeked out of my sleeping bag and tent and noticed the sky was clearing. I hurriedly dressed and leaped from the tent and filleted the walleyes that Bill and Denny caught while Steve, who crawled out after me, started the fire. After the fire was popping and the coffee perking, I called to the other voyagers, who were already squirming anxiously in their sleeping bags to join the morning ritual.

Mike was soon stoking the fire in his usual kneeling position, manning the fire and tending breakfast. The bannock dough was stirred and put along the coals for baking while we shoveled nutrition into ourselves. The bannock was done and stowed for lunch, camp was broken, and we were off again at 10:30 a.m.—a late start for us.

We had a great day of cranking through whitewater. We ran about six rapids marked on the topo maps and portaged around two falls or large rapids. From one of the portages, we stood in awe at some of the falls. Their beauty hides their power and danger. Sometimes we ran their zigzag route from one current tongue to the next. Sometimes we silently paddled along the edge in the softer current and snuck up on the rapids as if we were predators. But we always inspected the rapids before running them. We learned not to get cocky after Steve and I became swamped. Rapids are wonderful teachers. We preferred to run the rapids if possible because bushwhacking through the ancient overgrown portages infested with mosquitoes and blackflies was not one of our joys!

Steve and I wrestling through the rapids

We stopped paddling and shored up at a small island between two falls. Everyone silently attended to camp necessities, and while Mike made supper, Bill caught a beautiful brook trout. I envied his accomplishment but could not duplicate his success. I was looking forward to fly fishing tomorrow. After one of Mike's great meals,

Steve and I wrote in our journals, discussed the day's happenings, and planned tomorrow's goals. We planned to make Brassy Hill tomorrow, and then there should only be four more difficult rapids before we reached Hudson Bay. Looking down the river through the evening rapid's mist, I thought I could see Brassy Hill, and my insides began to quake. I was anxious to get the dangerous rapids through so we might relax again. I slipped out of my sleeping bag a couple of times during the night to watch the moonlight dance in the rapids and falls and to listen to the peaceful water message. But alas, I finally surrendered to my tent and dozed off with the song of the rapids dancing in my head.

Lee and Mike working through the hungry rapids

Bill and Denny dropping into the rapids

Moose Encounter!

July 23, 1983

We now felt accomplished and polished, a cohesive team. We could now reason rapids and calculate possible catastrophes. We planned our work and worked our plan with effective efficiency. We broke camp in a scurry and gulped a quick breakfast. But we hated to leave this idyllic island paradise. It was peaceful, beautiful, and fruitful with the bounty of brook trout. The thoughts were shattered by the sounds of the first rapids that we decided to run. And we did run it successfully.

Suddenly, in the foggy southeast, we could see Brassy Hill. It is the highest point in this part of Manitoba, the landmark assuring us that to finish the paddle to the bay would be shorter, faster, and safer than struggling back upstream to Oxford House if an emergency occurred. We pointed at the hill, shouted, then sighed with relief. This put us ahead of schedule because we thought we would not sight Brassy Hill until tomorrow, and here we were, after only an hour of paddling. Now the river flattened out with only a few threatening rapids with hungry rocks. We ran all the rapids except the last one, in which we lined the canoes around the periphery of the falls.

The welcome sight of Brassy Hill

At one of the rapids, Steve caught a nice (about three pounds) brook trout. Then Bill caught a nice one. Then I caught one. Then Mike caught one. Then Denny caught one. Then Lee caught one. We each caught one of the magnificent fish. They were all colorful and great fighters, but we limited ourselves to one fish each for Bill to fillet and fry for supper. The fillets were thick, red, and juicy and were a delight to our palate. We ate to our stuffed contentment.

Denny with our supper of brook trout

At one of the rapids, we had an interesting encounter. Descending the rapids and dodging boulders, we suddenly came upon a majestic bull moose who decided to cross the river right in front of us! We were on a collision course with the Sherman tank-sized ungulate and had no way to stop. Steve and I screamed, waved, and hammered our paddles on the water's surface in anxious excitement at the belligerent moose. I knew he saw us because he looked at us, perked his ears up, and pirouetted around back toward shore. I learned some time ago to judge moose by the body language of their ears. If their ears go up, they are alert and curious. If their ears go back, best look for cover or a tree to climb. My family and I were chased by a moose while backpacking in the Tetons once, and it wasn't a pleasant experience. We watched as the bull pirouetted and crashed through the dense forest, snapping alders and conifers carelessly as he lumbered irresponsibly. We saw the determined moose again about a mile down the river, crossing while looking at us with disgust.

We stopped at about 7:00 p.m. at another beautiful solitary island between two falls/rapids. We thought this might be the last barrier before reaching the bay but were not sure, just hopeful. This site was also extraordinary with our tent looking out over the stretch of the falls. The sights and sounds made it difficult to concentrate on sleep. But we finally went to sleep after another great brook trout dinner as the coals of the fire flickered and dimmed out. I was getting melancholy.

Boring Water

July 24, 1983

It was terrible! We all smelled like something that died in the swamp. As a matter of fact, I could not sleep most of the night because of the rank odor. At first, I thought it was Steve, but that was until I buried my head in my sleeping bag, only to discover it was me (also). So in the morning, we decided take a bath and clean ourselves up. At the downstream end of the island's falls, we found an inviting pool where we took turns bathing and washing our snarled hair and some of our smelly clothing. We also hung out our sleeping bags for an extra airing. It was invigorating and refreshing.

Dennis snoozing while drifting down the lifeless Hayes

We boarded our canoes and again started downstream. But everything changed. The rapids were gone, and we missed their challenging roar and the excitement of shooting through the rapids. Now all we saw were the barren clay banks and chocolate-colored water. The river became opaque like mountain lakes with glacial till. The conifers were replaced with scrubby krummholz-like groves of alder dwarf bushes. The rocky banks and azure-vermillion waters were disappointedly gone. The river was now benign and lifeless, now a milky white gray from clay erosion. The river was now placid and boring, not offering any challenge or providing drinking water. Expecting euphoria at the conclusion of the rapids, we became wary of the next three or four days of floating on an opaque Mississippi-like river in passivity.

Commiserating the Hayes

But then there was excitement. Coming around a bend in the river, we were suddenly upon a young bull moose who ventured midstream, stoically watching us. He was surrounded by our passing canoes and was not happy. He rebelled with some odd grunting sounds, and we quickly turned our heads to shore, looking for the mother to defend her young bull. He was standing belly-deep in the water, and we were afraid he might charge us. But he did not. We spoke softly to him, merrily chatted among ourselves, and took pictures, confident of our safety; and floated downstream past him.

Lee and Mike passing a young bull moose

We began to see more wildlife also, like ducks scurrying into the bulrushes and an immature golden eagle gracing the sky over us, almost in salutation. My, it was grand!

We stopped just short of the Fox River tributary, again on an isolated island, at about 6:30 p.m. We garnered clear water from the Fox, had supper, baked bannock, and went to sleep about 10:30 p.m. with the dreaded hum of the ever-present mosquitos.

Steve and I had a nightly hunt. After writing in our journals and watching the adopted spiders glean some of the mosquitos at the peak of the tent, we hunted the mosquito survivors with vengeful furor. I used my flashlight to highlight a mosquito on the inside of the tent, and Steve snatched and smashed them in his hands. It was a rewarding vigil we enjoyed every night. Steve had excellent dexterity and quickness in catching and dispatching the rascals—a skill I never mastered. We did not like to mash the blood-filled insects on the tent because we discovered the blood destroyed the waterproof fabric.

We were now in polar bear denning grounds and found their tracks as well as wolf tracks where we were camping, so we stacked pans on top of the food packs as an alarm system. And I kept the rifle at my side at the ready. I hoped I would not have to use the firearm, but if I did, I would send a warning shot first. I was uneasy as I struggled to sleep.

Gods River at Last

July 25, 1983

We arose at about 8:00 a.m. and quickly departed the mosquito-infested habitat without breakfast. The insects were like storm clouds descending upon us. After passing the Fox River inlet tributary, we stopped for breakfast on a windy point. The river was now quite wide, very milky colored, and moved fast but without rapids. It was bordered with rough eroded clay banks with twisted trees in grotesque shapes, threatening to grasp our canoes, motivating us to stay alert and near the center of the river. The trees at each corner of the river were scared from the ice going out during the spring thaw. The ice had cut through everything in its path like a giant buzz saw. In some places, we could see where the water and ice had been twenty feet or more high. We were glad we were not here a few months earlier.

The junction at Gods River was one of the last landmarks we needed to see before reaching Hudson Bay. And we made it. The Gods River somewhat parallels the Hayes, pours into the Hayes at this point, and forms a large placid yet toilsome eddy. Eric Severeid journeyed down the Gods River fifty years ago when he was a young lad and then wrote his inspirational book *Canoeing with the Cree*—the genesis of our odyssey.

We were somewhat disappointed when we reached the junction because we expected something special, perhaps a spiritual experience. It did not happen, but we were thankful to reach this point anyway. It was a pretty point that once supported a fort but was now totally gone. Despite our inspection, no remnants or artifacts were discovered. The Gods was just another big northern river slightly larger than the Hayes. Now the two of them merged to make a wide watery concourse.

It was now very warm and humid, so Lee and I went for a swim in the milky water, which was also warm but refreshing. We repossessed our canoes and continued downriver.

About two miles down the river, we discovered a neatly painted white cabin on a high bank. Upon investigation, we concluded that it was a Canadian hydrological monitoring station. Sadly, the screen doors and windows had been slashed and torn by ravaging bears trying to gain entry. There was a storm brewing, and the door was unlocked, so we decided to stay in the dry cabin for the night. This sounded like a good idea, but it was a mistake.

The hot and stuffy abode lacked intact screens, so Bill, Denny, and I patched together some screen material with duct tape to try and get some ventilation. We finally slid into our sleeping bags secure, warm, dry, and safe—or so we thought. Suddenly the storm broke over us at about 10:30 p.m. Torrential rain and wind blew into our makeshift screen barriers, and a multitude of mosquitos leaped upon the opportunity to banquet on us. The night was filled with cussing, slapping, rolling, and finally, laughter at our plight. Bill put on his woolies, head net, and all his repellant before propping himself in the corner to try to sleep. I finally discarded my sleeping bag in the sweltering heat, wrapped myself in the tarp/sail, and attempted to sleep. Others made curious attempts to cover themselves, but nobody slept much that sacrificial night.

Torture Aboard the Ship

July 26, 1983

Today was another mundane, boring day while floating down the vast slow-moving river with little useful current. We all had a terrible time through the stormy night with humming banshees sucking our blood, so we left in a scurried huff at daybreak—about 7:00 a.m. We were all bitten up, grumpy, tired, and hungry but glad to leave the place that looked so inviting.

We fixed all three canoes together with bungee cords but did not affix the sails because there was not a whiff of wind. Denny fired up his mountain stove in the aft of his canoe and fixed breakfast in passage. Each mile of the endless river seemed to be more boring than the last, with drab lifeless eroded shorelines and no drinking water. We have not seen any wildlife since entering the chocolate-milk water and were unable to procure drinking water since passing the Fox River. We assumed fishing would be poor, but we tried anyway and confirmed our suspicion. We were too tired and bored to even joke around, and Denny did not even tell any of his yarns. It was a quiet and lifeless drift.

At about noon, we decided to have lunch aboard the canoe-ship, and Denny was up to the task again. We did not want to shore up for fear of bears and insects, so we stayed onboard. We kept paddling slowly to give the impression that we were advancing, but we knew we were moving slowly under the hot sun. Some of us tried to sleep while one or two of the others attempted to keep us in the middle of the river, silently paddling. We slept in all sorts of contortions. Denny curled up in the fetal position in the bottom of his canoe. Steve and I lay backward on the packs in a head-to-head fashion. Mike, ever the intellectual, tried to read a book. We were all deliriously tired and burned out, like a group of shipwrecked limeys aboard a drifting life raft in the Atlantic. The blackflies, deerflies, and bulldogs attacked us relentlessly, but we fought back. I killed many with my glove in a flyswatter style and hit a bulldog using my paddle like a baseball bat. Once it cooled, the insects subsided, and the float became more tolerable.

Again, we stayed aboard and fixed a spartan supper aboard the linked canoes while drifting toward our goal: Hudson Bay. We finally put the canoe ashore at about 7:00 p.m. on a sandy island and retired after taking a well-deserved bath in the cool whirlpool-like shore. We were all chirping and excited about hoping to finally land at York Factory on Hudson Bay tomorrow.

Hudson Bay at Last

July 27, 1983

I awoke at 7:00 a.m. to rain tap-dancing on my tent—a discomforting awakening, and I discussed the dilemma with others. We decided to uncharacteristically stay in our warm sleeping bags until 10:00 a.m. I peeked out of our tent to see the disappointing slate-colored sky and realized it would be an all-day soggy vigil. Nevertheless, we ejected from out tents between cloud bursts, dismantled our wet tents, packed, policed the campsites, and departed unfed and damp with our canoes still strapped together. As usual, Denny manned his mountain-pack stove at his feet in the middle canoe and prepared a quick breakfast that we gulped with gratefulness. Steve and I paddled on one side while Bill and Lee paddled on the other, and Mike manned the rudder with his paddle. We all worked together at attempting to keep in the middle of the river, trying to stay in the rare current. We stopped occasionally for Bill and Denny to collect precious clear water from any tributary steam we encountered. Potable water was scarce.

We floated and paddled, mostly to feel useful, until we surprisingly saw a delightful euphoric site at which, despite being tired, we cheered with joy! In the foreground of the crystal-blue sky, waving to us was the Hudson Bay flag, almost like it was patiently waiting for us! It was a dashing red banner with the British Jack in upper left-hand corner and the HBC (Hudson Bay Company) initials in the lower right-hand corner. We later learned that the Cree thought the HBC meant "here before Christ" because the company preceded even the missionaries. We shored on the muddy bank just below the large white building just as a de Havilland Beaver was taxiing and leaving. We later learned that the plane was transporting the historic interpreter to the hospital. It appears she was ill with a sore throat and needed medical care.

Hudson Bay flag with the Union Jack

First sight of York Factory on Hudson Bay

Arriving at the bay

In addition to seeing the Hudson Bay Company's scarlet flag was the roof of the old warehouse with its lookout tower. The old building was dressed in a new coat of blazing-white paint. The blue sky greeted us, full of puffy white cumulus-cloud pillows. I fantasized a cannon salute for us, but it was only a natural phenomenon of low clouds often seen over the water. There before us was our goal: Hudson Bay—a body of water five times larger than the Persian Gulf that remains frozen until June each year. The water in the gulf is shallow and treacherous. At low tide, tips of boulders and mud flats are visible. Ships would only come in at high tide to be loaded, lest they run aground.

Running the canoes ashore in our excitement, we jumped out of our canoes and discovered that the shore was a wasteland of clay muck with the consistency of a chocolate malt—a gooey quagmire, and we all sank above our knees and looked at each other in anguish. It was a mess. Of course, we landed at low tide after the water had receded, as beckoned by the sun's and moon's gravity sometimes on the other side of the world.

We were met at the dock by Chris, a Cree, who was the "official" caretaker, but we did not see much of him after landing. It seemed he had other important details to attend and left us.

Shortly after, a distinguished older gentleman approached us and introduced himself as Doug MacLachlan. He was a most enchanting gentleman who wobbled, leaning on a cane in one hand and a leafy willow switch in the other to ward off insects. He wore a weathered but warm face, a white dress shirt, a black baseball hat, and high rubber boots for gleaning the shore during low tide for artifacts.

We later learned that Doug is retired and lives alone in his battery-powered cabin at York Factory and "looks after" the twenty or so paddlers who come through yearly. He said he had a wife in Winnipeg that he sees during the winter. Doug spoke with a heavy Scottish brogue accent and kept us entertained in the evenings until 11:00 p.m. with his tales of the Hudson Bay Company, First Nations People, and hunting escapades.

Doug cupped his hands and shouted over the wind to us, ordering us to pull our canoes and equipment up onto the upper shoreline. Landlubbers like us would have left the canoes mired in the chocolate soupy mess, only to be plucked out to sea by the high tide. The tide was forceful and dangerous. Doug explained that we were at low tide and that the high tide in a few hours would float our canoes and equipment out into the bay, never to be seen again. We complied and struggled to move everything to higher ground through the chocolate-malt mess. We were not familiar with tides in Minnesota.

Landing at low tide at the bay

A few hours later at high tide with canoes secured up the shore

We boldly asked Doug where to set up our tents and make camp. With a puzzled but firm look on his face, he slowly elevated his crooked tired cane à la magical wizard, pointed to a rustic red cabin, and proclaimed, "You'll be staying in the old red cabin," with his Scottish-Canadian gargling accent. "I don't think you'd want to sleep in your tents while you are here at the bay," he said as he pointed to the fresh dishpan-sized polar bear tracks. "I just scared him away with a shot in the air," he stated to reinforce his declaration and pointed to the inviting red cabin. We looked at each other, trying not to notice each other's knocking knees, then each one of us promptly picked up two packs and headed for the cabin posthaste.

The cabin was rustic but beautiful. It was decked with fake red brick siding and a grand green tar-paper roof. The outside doors and windows were trimmed in white paint and aggressive barbed wire to keep unwanted carnivorous guests out. The inside was even more astonishing, and we could not believe what we saw inside. There was a real table and enough chairs for our crew, six beds with real mattresses, and a gas stove and sink. Wow!

We dropped our packs and romped on claimed beds like a fresh batch of city kids at summer camp. After the celebration, we hung our damp clothes on the provided lines and set up the damp tents outside to dry. In the corner at the ready was a WWII vintage 8 mm

German Mauser to fend off marauding polar bears, lest they insist on entering the cabin.

Our red cabin with barbwire-guarded windows and Doug's cabin in the background

Barbwired windows to discourage polar bears

Mike could not wait to get at the gas stove and proceeded to inventory the cooking utensils available. The clatter of the pans was encouraging, and we could see joy on Mike's face. He soon had coffee perking for everyone, and we felt safe and secure. I took special joy in releasing the two accompanying spiders we adopted in our tent to help with mosquito control. Thanks, friends!

We then encountered a luxury we had not seen for some time—one all would need. It was a neatly appointed and decorated outhouse behind the cabin. It was such a pleasure to answer nature's call without embarrassment or tempting the mosquitos. The cabin was a palace to us even though it did not provide electricity or running water. Joy!

Drinking water was also an important commodity at the factory because the silt-laden water in the river and bay was not fit to drink. Ironically, here in this water wonderland, we had to scrounge for drinking and cooking water. Doug periodically collected water from a small stream that passed between the red cabin and the old cemetery and placed it into about twenty fifty-five-gallon metal drums beside his house. He then added some chemical to prevent algae and bacteria growth. It seemed to work because the water was crystal clear when we popped open the metal lid and dipped out our ration of water. However, we could see a few mosquito larvae swimming about at times.

The afternoon was spent searching for artifacts in the muddy low tide shoreline. Doug informed us that we could keep anything we found in the bay at low tide because it was fair game. That comment was motivational and sent us searching for artifacts for several hours while constantly glancing around for visiting polar bears. I carried the rifle as moral support. It was taboo to search or glean anything on shore. But at low tide, in the muddy flat, Steve found several interesting objects, including a swivel for a muzzleloader that he eventually gave to me. Lee found a large leg bone that he thought he might take home for Marylyn, his wife, thinking it was a moose bone. Mike informed us it was the right human tibia presumably washed up from an ancient Cree or voyageur grave. Lee reverently returned it to its watery gravesite. We found many objects, too numerous to mention, especially many handmade nails. Doug said that the nails were so valuable that when a York boat needed to be built, the old boat would be torched and the nails collected in the ashes to be reused. I excitedly found a great deal of flint and chert for knapping into igniters for my flintlocks back home. It was a sunny, muddy, fun outing. We took our treasures to the cabin to sort and share.

Mike with the human tibia Lee found at low tide

We finally managed to contact the girls back home through a patchwork system between Doug's shortwave and phone in Winnipeg. Through the crackly system, I told Donna, "At the bay, and everyone's okay… Let the other girls know." After the usual "I love you," the contact was lost, but I knew she got the message. The conversation was short and choppy with *over* after each sentence, but the voice at the end of the line was warm and special.

Most of the paddlers stayed up until 2:00 a.m. before retiring. I had a problem getting the crew to their sleeping bags because everyone was wound up and excited, chatting about the rewarding day. But things would change.

A HAYES RIVER ODYSSEY

York Factory Sojourn

July 28, 1983

It was a day of archeology and history! We spent the entire day with Doug, exploring the large antiquated York Factory building and combing the muddy beaches for artifacts. Both activities were enlightening and rewarding experiences.

The troops wanted to sleep late after staying up until 2:00 a.m., but I knew Doug would be at the cabin early in the morning to entertain us with more yarns and to give us the promissory grand tour of York Factory. So I rousted up the lads at about 7:45 a.m.—still late for us. Doug arrived shortly after, still clad in his "uniform," and off we departed for archival discoveries.

Doug chatted almost continually, chirping and pointing sometimes to one person, sometimes to us all, and sometimes to himself. He also asked questions as we progressed, almost like an experienced teacher to ensure that we were listening, and if he wasn't entirely sure about the function of some piece of equipment, he would quarry us. His cane was constantly poking at things and waving; he looked somewhat like a carnival barker, emphasizing to us a characteristic of some unknown implement. He was an interesting and fun performer to watch, riveting our attention. We listened intently and watched every move of his cane, lest we be inattentive, somewhat intimidated.

Doug lecturing on the importance of York Factory

York Factory was a huge square old building with a courtyard in the center for protection and to make transportation of hides and trade goods more efficient between areas of the factory across the courtyard. The construction of the factory was quite unique because it was built like an inverted ship with the roof trusses and supports like the thwarts and ribs of a vast ark. Naturally, all the lumber was hand hewn with axes, adzes, and saws, the marks till plainly visible. Most of the boards were tongue and groove and fitted nicely together, as sturdy as the day it was built. Doug explained that the roof was originally made of lead, so it must have been very heavy. The HBC packed almost everything in sheet lead, which could be reused and recycled easily. Lead is very malleable with a low melting point, so it can be made into other useful things like bullets and fishing weights. The floors were of loose, heavy plank construction, and beams were hinged to accommodate the change of the ground's contour with permafrost's undulating action. By manipulating wood wedges at the beam joints, the huge building could be maintained at a level status.

Entrance to York Factory with copula and boarded windows

Ship-like beam construction of York Factory

Worn latch and door of York Factory where a
multitude of voyageurs once entered

    The building was still guarded by a lonely cannon outside, overlooking the bay in a defensive manner. The supports were decayed, the barrel had a big chip at the muzzle, and a cannonball was stuck in the barrel. Nevertheless, it proudly leaned against the permafrost next to the fallen flagpole that once proudly lofted a red HBC banner so long ago. The canon reminded me of Doug, proudly leaning, except now the cannon was muted.

Steve and I mock-firing the cannon guarding the compound

Artifacts that had been collected by others in the past were displayed in the factory and organized according to their function or age along the walls on reconstructed counters or leaning against the wall. Each item, I was sure, would have its own story to tell. Doug, of course, could pretty much identify and explain where each item was found and what its function was. His recollection was uncanny. He was a York Factory encyclopedia.

Coins, lead bullets, buttons, and flints gleaned from the bay

Collection of cannons, cannonballs, anchors, and wheel hubs in the factory. Note the barbel-like projectiles intended to disable sail rigging as they spin.

The walls were especially intriguing in the old factory's main floor where pelts were sorted, pressed, and stacked. It seemed that each employee—whether British, French, or Cree—left their mark with a charcoal writing implement, like distant graffiti. Some left their names and dates, sometimes with a record of weights (perhaps of hides). Some left pictures—either self-portraits or of loved ones—or cartoonlike caricatures of their favorite clerk, the boss. Most of the writing was in the form of old-world drawn script. Apparently, Crees also toiled in the factory because there were petrographic-like drawings of caribou and moose as well as Cree cuneiform writings. The drawings were an intriguing art form I enjoyed.

When everyone left to congregate in another part of the factory, I stood, intrigued, alone in the large auditorium-like room. I squinted in the dim light to read the names and the dates and admire the artwork of the Cree, aided by shafts of light that struggled through the boards. I could almost hear the bustle of activity with hides being processed, obedient shoes shuffling along, and the clerk barking out orders. The atmosphere was ghostly, and I could almost hear footsteps following me out of the room. But it must have been just dusty echoes.

Some of the historic "graffiti" on the walls inside the factory

More wall "graffiti" art inside the factory

There was even a chapel with pews, stained glass windows, and a cross on the second floor. The pews looked like many voyageurs, boatmen, and Crees slid down them to worship. As Doug explained about the chapel reverently, it was obvious he spent many hours in prayer there.

The chapel inside York Factory

On top of the factory proudly stood an observatory copula. To reach the top required climbing a narrow stairway. The roof of the cupola contained signed names of other paddlers that had ventured down the Hayes or God Rivers. We lacked writing implements, so we were unable to register our names.

Signatures of previous paddlers on the ceiling of the cupola

After lunch, we spent the afternoon looking along the low tide muddy shores for artifacts under a cold and hazy sky. We found many treasures that we kept and a multitude of other interesting items that we left at the factory for others to enjoy.

We finally realized that our adventure was almost over and prepared to depart York Factory. Doug salvaged a slat from an old barrel in the factory for each one of us, fired up his propane torch, and, with the York Factory branding iron, made us each a special memento. He branded each of our paddles. We lined up and took our picture, packed our equipment, and made ready to make the final journey—or so we thought.

Doug branding our paddles with the York Factory brand

Lee, our dry leader, had made arrangements for an outfitter, John Hatley, to pick us up in shallow draft boats propelled by jetlike turbocraft motors to extract us from York Factory and to transport us up the Nelson River to Gillam, where we were to board the train for Wabowden and back to our vehicle. John was supposed to arrive about 2:30 a.m., so we retired early after doing the dishes, cleaning the floor, and burning the garbage. We wanted the cabin to be spotless for the next paddlers. Our packs were stacked and at the ready for a dash to the dock when John arrived. We were so busy we had neglected thinking or talking about our loved ones back home until now. We were all looking forward to squeezing our wives and family, and Steve his girl, now that it seemed possible. We were anticipating a special homecoming.

I awoke at 3:00 a.m. to an annoying "putting" noise. At first, I euphorically thought it was John's boat coming into the harbor. But it was the hopping coffeepot! Bill stayed up and was brewing the morning elixir for the departure. It was already late, and a storm was in full fury outside. The Canadian flag was stiffly stretched south by the north gale-force wind. Even the windows rattled warnings not to venture outside. There was pelting rain and opaque fog. We knew John would not make it, and we were again landlocked. We needed to wait out the storm, hoping John would eventually rescue us soon.

Marooned at York Factory

July 29, 1983

We spent the entire day watching the bay and hopefully expecting to hear the jet boats coming. We took turns sitting on the point below the outstretched flag in dark boredom, reluctant to discuss our plight with each other, only occasionally engaged in desultory conversation. After all the excitement of the rapids, this latent life was discouraging and depressing. When at the cabin, we took turns sprinting to the point with hope and trudged back in despair with our heads down. The fog continued to engulf the bay, and we knew we were in trouble. We tried to raise each other's spirits with humorous comments but to no avail; we had trouble cracking a smile.

We began retracing our previous York Factory tour by walking in and out of the factory, roaming around the grounds, and even going to Doug's house to see his extensive library of paperback books. Most of us could not even force ourselves to read.

We softly trod through the old cemetery again with solemn awe. There were a variety of headstones, most made of weathered wood planks with names and dates carved in or burned on their surfaces. Dates indicated there were many children that perished at York Factory. Life must have been hard and diseases prevalent, which probably claimed many of them. Most of the graves had wood picket fences neatly erected around their site, and the "factors," who were the chief bosses, and clerks had granite makers and metal fences.

Supposedly, even in death, there was a hierarchy. Doug explained that the fences were to discourage wolves and bears from unearthing the succumbed. We picked no artifacts from the sacred place.

The day dragged on with no rescue in site. Finally, we retired to our bags, wondering about tomorrow.

The author considering our maroon dilemma

Decision Time

July 30, 1983

We watched the clock closely because high tide usually came in twelve-hour shifts plus an hour. And high tide was the only time that John would be able to get here because of the shallow bay. After the crest of the high tide at 3:00 a.m., it was obvious John would not be able to make our rendezvous until about 4:00 p.m., so we slept late. I arose at 8:00 a.m. and slogged to the point. The fog was still there, hovering over us like an evil spell. The bay was socked in fog and windy. I returned to the cozy cabin dejected and nudged indoors by the cold north wind. I was expecting to report the weather to the lads, but I was greeted by buzzing, snorting, and whistles of sleeping voyagers. I decided to spend the time refining my journal and sipping coffee made with reused grounds. Doug arrived shortly after my last journal entry, making his usual morning appearance.

Lunch was special. Doug treated us to a savory lunch of fried caribou meat he had recently harvested. It was tender and tasty and especially good because Doug accompanied the meal with a prayer of thanks for bringing the paddlers, as he called us, to York Factory. He always liked to join us for our meals even though he did not always eat with us because, as he explained, "I like your prayers before your meals." Lunch was also special because Mike and Lee smuggled in some small plastic toys to share with each paddler. The good food, prayer, and gifts raised our spirits. We giggled and laughed as we fondled the miniature cars and trucks in the festive atmosphere.

Bill and Mike opening "presents" at lunchtime

Quickly after lunch, we again scurried around, cleaning the cabin again, packing our equipment, and prepping the canoes. We were sure John would be here to pick us up at high afternoon tide because the weather seemed to be clearing. The sun was ablaze, and we were looking forward to seeing seals, walruses, and beluga whales in the bay. It was going to be a great trip, possibly with some fishing stops included. There was an air of giggly excitement as we struggled to wait like children at Christmas Eve.

Then we waited and waited and waited some more. But John never came. The bay was still foggy and windy, and we were not encouraged. A floatplane came in, and the pilot reported that the weather was terrible on the Nelson River where John was stranded. The Nelson is a large river that drains into the bay some miles north of us. We considered canoeing north and then up the Nelson to Gilam, paddling our canoes, but Doug discouraged the idea. He explained that it was dangerous because we could become lost in the fog on the bay. He said a group some years ago tried and were never heard from again. We aborted the idea and decided to painfully wait. The Nelson also has a large dam across it that is sometimes opened unannounced—another potential problem. We now became concerned about John's safety. Reality struck us, and we slowly trickled back to the docking area and dejectedly recovered our packs. We were marooned again, except this time it was worse because we were now almost out of food. We watched as the wind tore at the flag and thoughts gravitated home.

To break the monotony, most of us went artifact hunting again. And we all found more treasures, but our eyes and thoughts were mostly on the Nelson River to the north. When would the fog lift and wind cease?

Suddenly, at about suppertime, the wind switched to a more easterly direction, and the fog slowly lifted. We wanted to rejoice but knew better because it could change at any moment and redirect from the north again. Bill seemed most disappointed because he had not seen Vicki for six weeks, and the loneliness was evident even through the fog-and-wind-filled agony. One important thing we learned through this expedition is that weather dictates what you wear, where you go, and when you travel. Forcing the situation can exasperate an already dire situation. After mildly venting our frustration, we settled down back at the cabin or on the steps, reading some of Doug's old *Reader's Digest*s, writing in our journals, and writing poetic letters that we could hopefully send from Gilam—someday!

For supper, Mike whipped up a magical gastric delight from some scrounged peas, corn, and Lipton soup another group left behind in the cabin. It was as good as ever with Mike's great magic chef's touch, and we all complimented Mike on his skills. He was filled with pride.

Surprise! After supper, Doug burst in and announced that six other paddlers just arrived from Minnesota. They were all wide-eyed young chaps from Minneapolis who started at Cross Lake and came through Oxford Lake also. They came in two canoes with a "duffer" sitting on top of the packs in the middle. They were wet, cold, and hungry, so we treated them to hot coffee and leftovers before sending them upstairs to the other bunks to settle in. Doug returned out of breath with his branding iron. He quickly branded their paddles and whisked them off to the factory for a tour before nightfall engulfed them. There were no lights, lanterns, or electricity at the factory, so the tour would have to be quick. Doug planned to go to Gilam with us on the jet boats, so he wanted to do as much as possible for the youthful paddlers before he left.

Then the torturous waiting renewed. To pass the time, we read more ancient *Reader's Digest*s Doug had accumulated, wrote more journal entries, letters, and postcards, and just mournfully chatted. But mostly, we just waited and silently prayed for our suffering to cease. Then we waited some more. Occasionally, one of us would slog dejectedly to the point and strain our ears to hear the expectant angelic music of John's boat motor, but it was all in vain. All we could hear was the whistling wind. We surmised that John was probably still stranded somewhere out in Hudson Bay, so at 3:00 a.m., we decided to retrieve our packs from the point, unpack our sleeping bags, and try get some sleep. No sooner had we lay down than Steve rushed into the cabin with arms aloft and with fingers in the victory shape as he breathlessly shouted, "I told you they'd be here!" We jumped into our shoes and dashed out under the bright full moon and dazzling northern lights. Everything seemed more beautiful. Bill grabbed his pack and dashed back down to the flagpole point. I was a close second, only to hear John and his partner cussing out in the bay about the fog and wind. It was obvious our Olympic efforts were wasted. I anxiously shouted through the fog, asking when we might leave. John shouted back between cuss words, "Not until the next high tide!" That would be in twelve hours. We pirouetted in utter disappointment and silently returned, dejected, back to the cabin. I simply fell on top of my sleeping bag and slumbered fully clothed.

Change in Plans

July 31, 1983

We awoke at about 8:00 a.m. to the sound of Mike stoking up the coffeepot, and soon the tantalizing aroma of coffee filled the cabin. After an improvised breakfast, John came up to the cabin and informed us that he arranged with Gilam Airline for them to pick us up. This would allow him to take the other group and Doug with his boats back to Gilam and put him back on schedule. He had another party to pick up on Wednesday and did not want to risk another weather delay.

John left at 1:00 p.m. with the young chaps and Doug. Chris went fishing, and suddenly we were at York Factory alone without transportation, communication, or a guide. It was kind of a lonely wait primarily because Doug was gone. We always felt secure when he was around, but now even he had abandoned us. We felt grim and subdued and alone at Hudson Bay.

We took the packs and canoes to the main dock where the planes would come in. Then we went back to the cabin to wait some more. I went out to the point several times to listen for the drone of the airplane motors, but all I could hear was the drone of mosquito wings. Once, I thought I heard the sweet mechanized motor music and dashed to get Denny to listen with me. But he just looked out of the corner of his eyes oddly and sternly shook his head with a negative gesture.

Denny and Steve waiting for the planes to arrive

York Factory dog accompanying us to the dock

Then, at about 3:30 p.m., we suddenly heard the thunder of the de Havilland Beaver and the Cessna 185 blaze past the cabin to check the landing area in the bay. We grabbed our cameras and hats and sprinted down to the shore's edge in a helter-skelter fashion like a rescued bunch of castaways. The pilots deftly taxied the planes to the dock, and we secured the planes and lashed the canoes to the pontoons with nervous hands. We then filled the cockpits with equipment as we followed orders from the youthful pilots. But I was concerned. Both pilots were young, and upon questioning, one said this was his first flight with clients while the other said he had never flown with a loaded floatplane before. But then I become more relaxed when the older pilot barked out orders with authority to us and the other pilot. He directed us to pile all the heavy materials up close to the engine in the copilot area. He explained that this would put most of the weight close to the power of the engines, helping with liftoff. And he also directed the younger pilot to direct the nose of the plane into the wind to artificially increase the air speed and assist with liftoff. I felt better.

With a flick of the starter switch, the engines roared to life, and I watched and prayed as I saw the spray disappear under the pontoons as we taxied out to the bay. The pilot pushed the throttle forward, and the motor roared louder. I could feel the strain on the engine as we lifted and leveled off. The pilot was quite clever because he tilted the plane slightly to break the meniscus of the water's surface one pontoon at a time as we lifted off. We struggled up and away. Good job!

And back up the Hayes River we went, except this time we were airborne and going upstream into the wind before turning toward Gilam, our flight destination. Because we put most of the weight toward the engine, I lay unstrapped on top of the heavy packs in the copilot seat. I rolled around a bit, but I had a great view of the topography and our river. The air in the stuffed cockpit was like an incubator turned sauna, but we were glad to be on our way.

The Hayes River heading upriver from the air to Gilam

After a one-and-half-hour smooth flight, we dropped nicely into a small lake on the edge of Gilam where a major disappointing dispute evolved.

The airport manager charged into our group like a raging bull and proceeded to swear profanities at us and the pilots. We were dismayed and did not know what was going on. He made it clear that he didn't like Americans by the tenor of his voice. He was upset because we had not paid in advance to be picked up. He scolded the pilots and insisted that they should have left us stranded on the bay. But then I was impressed with the older young pilot. He looked the manager in the eye and sternly said, "Be real. These guys were in trouble, and we had to get them out of there!" I nearly lost it, but Lee calmly stepped in and diplomatically tempered the situation with a calm tone and arranged for the flight cost to be covered by the funds John, with the jet boat, was originally entitled to. The manager reluctantly agreed but then charged us $20 to drop off our equipment at the motel and canoes at the train depot—a short distance. The pilots agreed to do it for free, but the manager insisted on $20 for the use of his truck. We scratched together $20, and Lee politely placed the funds into the red-faced manager's hand. It was an uncomfortable and ugly experience.

Arriving at Gilam and civilization from York Factory

Civilization at last! We dropped the canoes off at the train depot and checked in at the motel. A shower, a TV, a telephone, electric lights, and soft beds were all here in the civilized world, but so were wanton litter, dirty streets, and a drunken group fighting outside our window. But then, I guess they are part of the world also. We all showered, put on our cleanest dirty clothes, and prepared to go out for dinner. We had not eaten a real meal for some time, so we were famished. Wes and Mark, the two young pilots, were great chaps and later met us in town for dinner. They were more mature and empathetic than the manager and tried to settle the manager down but with limited success. It was great getting sustenance into our bodies, elevating our energy and attitude.

We had to catch the train at 1:00 a.m., so that meant another night without sleep. We stayed up to not oversleep and to do our final packing. Lee reserved a boxcar for our canoes and packs. I was hoping there would not be any more conflicts.

Riding the Rails

August 1, 1983

It had been a long time since I had ridden in a train, and this bumpy rail trip was especially enlightening. The train arrived at 1:05 a.m., right on time, and we needed to quickly and efficiently load the canoes and gear into one end of the assigned boxcar—this, after the conductors gathered and discussed who had the most seniority and thusly in charge. They huddled and discussed their credentials in a polite mood. Finally, they emerged like a football team with one of the older conductors like a quarterback emerging, giving orders with arm-waving directions.

He directed us to our boxcar where the canoes were stacked, fully loaded with our packs and gear, piggyback in one end of the boxcar to save room for other scheduled cargo in the other end. We noticed Doug in one of the cars frantically waving to us. After some coercion, the conductor let us on to visit Doug. He was in the smoking section, so we just said hi and walked and coughed to the other end of the passenger car. We intended to go back and visit with him, but when we returned, he was asleep. It did not matter where we sat because all the Cree in the car were smoking heavily anyway. It was truly a stifling experience.

While boarding the train, we were quite shocked at the toilsome crowd we witnessed. The night's darkness seemed to open, and countless Cree emerged. It was quite sad because most of them were totally inebriated. And the intoxication was not limited to the adults. Usually, the entire family was drunk, including some of the children. They usually clung to each other and leaned on each other in a futile attempt to attain stability and direction. One sad case I witnessed was a young boy who was disabled and seemed to be intoxicated was trying to board the train. His mother, who also was drunk, tried in vain to help him board. I felt helpless, not knowing if I should interfere and try to assist. Before I decided to reach out to help, one of the compassionate conductors came to the rescue; he picked up the helpless lad and took him to a seat. He quickly returned to help the mother board and seat also. I was quite impressed at the patience and politeness of the conductors as they attended to the Cree. Many of them did not have tickets, and the conductor would dig into their pockets and billfolds to retrieve the cost of a ticket and nicely return the containers. The conductors were very firm and direct but polite and service-minded. The passenger cars, as well as the boxcar, were tidy and clean also. I was impressed.

Loading canoes and equipment on boxcar at Gilam at 1:00 a.m.

Sitting across the aisle and several seats back from us was a group drunk, smoking, and swearing. The only words we could understand were the graphic swear words. We were quite uncomfortable, but we did not say anything to them. Although we were offended, we were too tired to vocalize. Thankfully, one of the conductors, a fine-boned, red-haired, bucktoothed younger man went back and scolded them like a parent chastising misbehaving children. He even threatened to remove them from the train before they finally settled down. But when the conductor left and went to the patrol the next car, the gaiety resumed, deluging us with sleeplessness until the poor souls fell asleep.

I looked at our paddlers and was quite entertained with the different sleeping positions they considered comfortable. Steve put his red bandana over his eyes to eliminate some of the light. Others buried their heads in some undescriptive manner to filter out some of the sounds and smoke, keeping them from offending their bodies. I finally buried my head in my jacket and succumbed to needed rest.

After some time, I awoke to a jolt. In a daze, I looked about. We were in Thompson, and the Cree exodus was on. Most of them that slept were now somewhat sober, but some stumbled along with the crowd like misdirected sheep. The passenger car was now vacant except for us paddlers, quiet except for the sleeping serenade of my comrades. Suddenly I thought of Doug! I looked over at his seat, and it was empty. Then I remembered he said he was going to visit friends in Thompson. I hurriedly glanced out the window and saw him melt into the early morning Cree humanity. He never looked back, probably assuming we all were still asleep. But that was Doug's style. He was not one for long goodbyes.

I did not realize until after he disappeared that I had met a special person. He was not special because he was a literary genius (although, he was well-read). He was not special because he amassed a great deal of financial wealth (although, he was rich with memories, which he shared). But he was special because he danced to his own music, especially the north country music that embraced him. He had his own ideas, stimulated by the north, of how he should live and did not allow riches or materials tempt him. Once, while talking in the cabin, he very emphatically said, "I have no need of money. What good would money be to me?" He told us that he was offered a job by a wealthy family visiting York Factory just because their children liked him. He said no because he had everything he wanted. And he did. Now, do not get me wrong. Doug wasn't a hermit. He loved people and conversing with them. But it was obvious his values were different than those of most. This is what separates people. The tenor of his voice resounded with his love for the earth and the one who made it. He recognized his faults and submitted to forgiveness. To me, he was a special twentieth-century hero, and I am grateful I had the opportunity meet him. I will never forget him.

After a successful scouting mission from car to car, the length of the empty train, Lee found and sampled breakfast in the dining car that we did not know existed. He returned to our car and reported his finding warm breakfast food. The rest of us scrambled and wobbled our way to the dining car, trying to anticipate the sway and bumps of the railroad, to gain nutrition. The waitress greeted us and assigned us seating. She was a shapely, stern young gal with a defensive, stiff lower lip. She had straight hair and a frigid personality. I felt like I should click my heels and snap to attention as she directed us to sit, and we did. Then she turned to me and barked, "Take off your lid!" I immediately jerked off my hat as directed, and I clicked my heels under the table and had to restrain a formal salute. We each ordered either eggs or pancakes. I selected eggs, which only came scrambled. Mine were medium to rocky and would have made a great racquetball. Otherwise, the coffee and service were great. I was impressed with the Canadian National Railroad.

We screeched to a halt in Wabowden at about noon. Bill and I guarded the canoes and equipment while the rest of the crew went to get the rusty van (yellow snow pile) and trailer and to negotiate with George at the airport. There seemed to be some disagreement between the two fly-in services as to what the plane load capacities were. The capacities were important because the loads determined the transport fee. It cost us about $400 more to fly with George going in, so a clarification was necessary. But the discussion with George was fruitless. His charts indicated that he was correct, hence the charges remained intact, and the refund we erroneously requested was not justified.

While Bill and I waited at the rail station, I chatted with an older female science teacher from Thompson who was waiting at the station. She elaborated very enthusiastically about the curriculum at her school, and she gave me her analysis of the Cree problem in Canada and of how to solve their plight. She was quite verbal, and I did not have the opportunity to share the merits of Mayo High

School curriculum in Rochester. It was a fun one-way chat, and I enjoyed listening.

The crew, the Chevy suburban, and the trailer finally got back to the rails, and we loaded all the packs into the trailer and canoes on the overhead trailer rack carefully for the last leg of a long journey.

Down the bumpy road in the wired-up Chevy suburban we flew. We were all quiet and melancholy, knowing an exciting voyage was over. We were lost in canoe memories and dreams of linking with our friends and families back home.

We made several gas stops and tried to have supper at the Chicken Delight restaurant, which was nearly empty. The effort was wasted because we were evicted by an angry older waitress who claimed she had "too many pizzas to make." With a scrawny bent finger, she directed us to the Gulf gas station down the road. We politely left hungry and dejected.

At the gulf station, we engaged in another controversy involving a confused waitress and an angry cook, which almost resulted in another eviction. After explaining how hungry we were, the waitress seated us under the metal steps like second-class citizens, and we finally had dinner after a one-and-a-half-hour wait. Our impatience was overcome by our hunger. We humbly ate and commented how we missed Mike's cooking.

Home at Last

August 2, 1983

> The magic thing about home is that it feels good to leave, and it feels even better to come back.
> (Wendy Wunder)

During the odyssey, I often thought about home but tried to shun worry because there was little I could do to rectify any theoretical problems. Now as we drove south toward home haven, my heart and mind began to wonder in earnest:

"Are Donna and the kids okay?"

"What about Josie, my springer?" Does she miss me?

"How did Donna cope with everything at home while I was gone?"

"Who mowed the lawn?"

"Do our old cars work okay?"

"Did I get any important calls?" Whenever I am gone, Donna always has a list of calls for me to return.

Then my thoughts turned to school, which was about to start:

"What is my schedule going to be?"

"How many students will be in each of my classes?"

"How many sections of biology or environmental studies will I have?"

"Who will my students be?"

And on and on I labored through introspection.

On and on, the suburban rumbled on inerrantly down the bumpy road, through customs, and down Minnesota roads until we reached Rochester at about 12:30 p.m. and the joyous arms of loved ones. It was great to be back to civilization and the comforts of city living, but part of us will always stay at York Factory. It was difficult to believe that just two days earlier, we were stranded on Hudson Bay, locked in by fog. And today we were home with our loved ones, unscathed by mosquitos, bulldogs, and blackflies. Would the odyssey have a lasting effect on us? Or would we take the experience for granted? Or was it just a recreational endeavor with a cohesive group of men? Only time and some changes in our attitudes would eventually tell. Time judges all. Any experience is a wasted experience if it does not have a lasting positive change in our attitude and values.

Chapter 10

The Daily Routine

Having a routine, knowing what to do, gives me a sense of freedom and keeps me from going crazy. It's calming.
—Chuck Close

Routines are comforting. Routine establishes rhythm to an effort and cohesiveness among the participants. Like a well-oiled gearbox, the gears are incorporated into a working unit to complete a necessary driving task. Essential to this routine is the division of labor and responsibilities to the people involved. Some erroneously think that leadership involves doing everything and accepting all the responsibilities in attaining a goal. Good leadership involves finding the strengths of each member of the effort, assigning the responsibility to that individual, and giving them the freedom to pursue their responsibility as they see fit. Good leaders do not do everything and micromanage but should know all the aspects of the assigned responsibilities. There should be a melodious rhythmic hum to the effort with few controversies. There are instances when, by design, other members of the party's decisions supersede the overall leader's jurisdiction. Speed and safety are enhanced by efficiency.

Safety is always paramount. And this routine also enhances group safety. Safety and efficiency go hand in hand, especially in such an endeavor as our Hayes River Odyssey. If everyone knows their responsibility and what the other members' responsibilities are, then everyone knows just about where everyone is and what they are occupied with. This "sixth sense" gives each member of the team confidence. Nothing, especially speed, should limit safety. We all felt confident in each other and relied on each other's expertise. This was a joyful cohesive group to work with. We were a well self-disciplined team.

When efficiency and safety are maintained, then enjoyment can be experienced. If each member of the party knows their responsibility and can perform their tasks to their maximum efficiency, then they usually will complete their tasks quickly and efficiently so that they might have more time for enjoyment. This was evident in our group because everyone would be scurrying around to complete their tasks so they might have time to read, write in their journals, or go fishing. Enjoyment in our case was a reward for a job well done and deserved. Without appropriate responsibility completion, enjoyment might be limited.

Here is how the day usually went, with some modifications dictated by weather. I would usually awake about 5:00 a.m. with the first bird chirping in the morning dawn. I have programmed myself to awake in this manner and enjoy waking up early. If I needed to arise earlier, I'd usually drink two sierra cups of water just before reclining. Then my bladder became my dependable alarm clock.

Immediately after awaking, I would check my pocket watch next to my air mattress to check the time and say good morning to my wife's picture inside the cover before winding the watch and snapping close the lid. Then I would look outside the tent with anticipation to check on the weather, especially the wind and the threat of mosquitos. If it was raining, I would go back to my sleeping bag and let the lads continue their slumber until 8:00 a.m. For several days, we slept until 10:00 a.m. while a storm rumbled over us. Usually, it would storm at night and build during the day. If it became hot and humid after a shower, then it would usually storm viciously later during the day. If the mosquitos were drumming on the tent and awaiting us, I would clamber about the tent to clothe myself with protection, including my head net and gloves. Before unzipping the tent and crawling out, I would uncork my air mattress so it might deflate by itself and spread my sleeping bag out to air it.

If we camped on a lake (usually on an island) and intended to sail in the morning, upon arising, I would check the wind direction and speed. If both were favorable, I would roust the crew with haste to not miss the opportunity for leisurely travel. With the desirable wind conditions, we would usually postpone breakfast until we were sailing, pushed by the benevolent wind. Once stabilized, Denny would fire up his pack stove in the stern of his canoe, and we would eat breakfast on the move. This saved time and helped us escape the intolerable mosquitoes awaiting us on the shore.

If it was a paddle day, then I'd get up and start a fire or have Steve, who was my tent partner, start Denny's stove; and we'd have aromatic coffee and hot water for the morning cereal and prunes for the crew before we awoke them. If Mike did not arise, motivated by the clatter of the cook kit, he would carefully leave out the planned breakfast menu with instructions. We would carefully follow the recipe because we knew Mike's meal pride.

We would usually lay out our next day's clothing before retiring. Often, they would be the same gamy garments we wore the day before, so little preparation was necessary. We would try to wear clean underwear if available, but that, too, was often optional. I usually used my clothing as a pillow, which I considered comfortable, and it would be warmed by my head, ready for me to don in the morning chill. I liked my wool Paul Pezolt shirt (he gave it to me many years ago at a climbing workshop) next to my head. Our head nets and gloves were strategically placed inside the tents near the door to grab for protection when we exited the tent; this was to prevent the hordes from attaching to our faces and hands. After determining that the surrounds were conducive, I would dress, stuff my sleeping bag into the stuff bag, and roll up my uncorked air mattress. Then I would place the sleeping bag, mattress, air pump, flashlight (after reversing one of the batteries), and candle lantern into the watertight bag. I considered this my most important bag and made every attempt to ensure that the contents stayed dry. Donning my head net and gloves, I would toss out my treasured bag and scurry out of the tent, quickly zipping it closed.

The percolating coffee and the clatter of vittles being made usually rousted up the rest of the crew, and they would be ready to eat and paddle.

After breakfast, it would be time to tend the tent. We always tried to set our tents so that the morning sun would strike it early to evaporate any moisture that might have accumulated on the rainfly. If it was impossible to set the tent in the predetermined desirable location, then the rainfly would be removed and placed in the sun to dry on the bushes while we ate breakfast.

I determined that the sun came up at about fifty-two degrees from the north on the first day, so each evening, we could pretty much determine where the sun's rays would come up. Nevertheless, the tents were rolled up immediately after breakfast and secured in the appropriate packs even if damp. We could dry them later, if necessary.

Everyone would then tend to his own pack, and everything had its place. We usually placed everything inside a large heavy plastic bag before sealing it and putting it into our Duluth packs. Rain gear and head nets were always packed near the top for rain and insects that often infested portages.

Each canoe carried three packs and other equipment. Two of the packs, of course, were personal packs, and the third was a food and equipment pack. Each canoe also held two tubes lashed to the thwarts nested next to the gunwale and contained the busy fishing rods, protecting them from breakage. Two extra paddles, a bailer or sponge, a fish lip gaff, and a waterproof camera box or bag for each paddler was also included. Mike and Bill, our two physicians, also carried their elaborate first aid kits in separate canoes. The precious cook kit always came through the rapids in the last canoe. The first aid kits and the cook kit were essential and guarded.

After all the equipment is loaded into the canoes, we'd run a light cord through all the pack straps so if the canoe were to flip upside down, the contents would stay in the canoe and wouldn't become lost. The packs, with locked air, also added buoyancy to the rig. Then the contents were covered with a large spray skirt for protection from rain and threatening standing waves as we cascaded through rapids.

We placed heavier lines stern and aft on the canoes as running lines. These were checked and monitored often and used if we had to jump out in the rapids and line the canoe along shore or tie up to shore quickly or in case of a turnover (to hand to a rescuing canoe). Mike and I also carried throwing buoys to aid a paddler who might drift downstream without his canoe.

If any whitewater, rapids, or even riffles were to be run, life jackets were mandatory. We would not take any chances. If the water was placid, we would take our jackets off but keep them at hand. Denny, because he was in the last canoe, would check the campsite before we left so nothing was left behind and that we left the forest tidy. Anything we did not burn was carried out. After getting the thumbs-up from Denny, we would disembark.

We usually tried to cover as much water as possible in the cooler mornings. Running downriver took little effort except for when we cranked in the rapids, dodging boulders and an occasional moose. When possible, sailing gave us the opportunity to be together and chat. It was also an opportunity to monitor everyone's attitude.

At about noon, we would have lunch. Bill would prepare the lunch in advance either the night before or during breakfast when the bannock was baked and the lunch packed in a Charles Chips can. It was a cold and quick but nutritious meal, and we would either land on a rocky point or an island or hook up our canoes together side by side to eat lunch and commiserate. Lunch time was always a good and relaxing time to check the maps and to stretch out atrophied bodies.

After lunch, we would press on again with a vengeance to subdue the water's wrath. We tried to keep moving lest we fall behind schedule even more. We would pull, push, and crank through the waters and try to gain as much distance as possible before night. We usually found an accommodating island or point by 8:00 p.m. Windy islands were ideal to frustrate mosquitoes and blackflies, our nemeses.

The tents were set up posthaste so that if a storm broke, we would have someplace to scurry to. Usually, the sail was erected as a dining fly and a clothesline strung out to accommodate drying items and sometimes to air out sleeping bags. Once air mattresses were filled with soft air, they were placed in the tents with unfurled sleeping bags atop in an inviting position. We were usually exhausted, and it was tempting to just crash into soft repose. Making the "house" ready was always a top priority.

Then it would be time for dinner. Denny would get out his trusty folding saw and get firewood neatly stacked and ready. Mike would have the tinder ready, and soon vittles were vibrating on the unfolded fire grate. I fabricated a folding fire grate to cook on and to not make objectionable fire rings. Now we could relax a bit and dine on one of Mike's gastric, filling delights.

After dinner, two people usually volunteered to do the dishes. The cook, usually Mike, did not scrub dishes, so he could attend some of his personal tasks. We all liked to do the dishes because it was an opportunity to get our hands really clean. The dish soap and warm water was soothing to the hands and felt luxurious. Although, it did make our hands softer and more vulnerable to blisters when we pressed through the rapids. After the dishes were cleaned and stacked on a boulder or log to dry, we had time to relax, groom ourselves, and go fishing.

After a hard day of paddling, there was nothing more refreshing than a swim, bath, and shampoo. We would take turns frolicking in the shallows by ourselves in the nude. We felt totally unencumbered. We tried our best not to use too much soap to limit phosphate pollution. Being camped near a rapids or on an island between rapids provided a cool whirlpool that was physically and emotionally therapeutic.

Fishing was always great. We found that anything shiny tossed into the rapids resulted with a piscatorial gift. Northerns were the easiest to catch, but they were boney and had teeth like an alligator. They came in various sizes, but we harvested very few of them. They were voracious fighters and fun to catch and release. Walleyes were the best for eating and were cooperative biters in the rapids. Brook trout were my favorite and could easily be caught on a fly or jig with a fly rod. They had thick shoulders and were juicy, some in the three-pound range. We also caught whitefish that were very good, but they were harder to catch. I had to keep reminding myself that this was not intended to be a fishing trip but that fishing was adjunct to the canoeing adventure. Sometimes the fish were used as part of our dinner or kept on a stringer for breakfast. We would try to catch and keep one husky fish for ourselves and release others just for the joy of catching the beautiful creatures. We all knew we would become spoiled by the wonderful fishing experience.

After dinner, we did not sit around the fire and sing songs or play the harmonica. Upon landing, we would efficiently set up camp with little being said. Everyone tended tasks without consultation or conflict. The same would occur after dinner. Things needed to be done, and tents were awaiting slumbering voyagers. If there was any talk, it was somber and sober.

There was no curfew except when the embers were at their glowing deaths, then they were ceremoniously drowned with river water. This was the signal to get rested for tomorrow's challenges. We usually retired at about 10:00 or 10:30 p.m. Steve and I would lie on our sleeping bags, light our candle lanterns, and write in our journals. Sometimes we would also study the maps and schedule the next day's events and calculate how far we should plan to paddle. I would also read my Bible and say good night to my wife's photo hidden in the lid of my pocket watch and take one more look at the sky before extinguishing the candle lantern and finally lying down. During the day, I always looked forward to this time of silence, meditation, solitude, and my soft inviting sleeping bag.

Chapter 11

Running the Rapids

Choose to chance the rapids & dare to dance the tide
—Garth Brooks

Running the rapids was the most enjoyable, enlightening, and thrilling aspect of the voyage but also sometimes the most dangerous to encounter. So we took special precautions to ensure safety and to enhance enjoyment. Each rapids held an unfolding drama to be experienced and required fearless gallantry.

Rapids are an interesting phenomenon. Character is made up of features that distinguish an individual, like traits that mark an individual. And personality includes the disposition and temperament—the dominate quality/trait/mood/attitude of the individual.

We learned that each rapids had its own character and personality and that, by listening and observing from the upper limits, we could determine what kind of character we were dealing with and what its personality and mood were. Some were benevolent and easy to understand while others were vocal, chaotic, and threatening. Nevertheless, they needed to be encountered and conquered. We would gather to strategize our battle plan sometimes from shore and sometimes while gliding back and forth at the head of the moat to select our route. Usually we would fairy-glide across the mouth of the of the rapids, almost like teasing a monster, to look for the invitational *V* or tongue, which would usually be the desirous route. Often, the thoughts of entering the beast's mouth chasm knotted our entrails. But it had to be done.

Steve and I had the most experience with whitewater, so we led most of the threatening cauldrons. Steve usually knelt in the bow, covering his lower body with the front spray skirt, and I sat or knelt in the stern. As we entered the chaotic water, I would intently watch and listen to Steve because he could see best. We were followed by Mike and Lee and finally by Denny and Bill with the cook kit. The rule was that if Steve and I did not make it through the rapids, they should try an alternative route or attempt portaging around the rapids.

If no route could be established, then we'd "turn invertebrate" and search for a portage. Other members of the party also helped look for a safe land passage to the lower end of the rapids, which usually proved strenuous. If a portage was found, then Steve and I would trek the trail and look for an accommodating water route. We learned that once a portage, usually an old trail, was found, it usually meant that it should be used. As the Crees would say, "There never was an Indian who drowned on a portage," which was a wise adage. If Steve and I thought the rapids could be run, we would gather the team at the mouth and enlighten the other two canoes about the proposed route. Then Steve and I would run the rapids with Steve shouting, "Right," or, "Left," usually in rapid succession while my heart pummeled in my chest, and I would respond with quick strokes to elude hungry rocks. Often, I could not hear Steve well above the roar of the water, so I'd watch Steve's strokes. His draw or crossbow stroke dictated where we should go and what stroke I should use to dodge mishaps and maintain a downstream canoe attitude.

Steve and I would gather our canoe and thoughts in the friendly eddies at the end of rapids and signal with a wave of a paddle for the next group to proceed. It was always a relief to glide into swirling eddies and signal the next group. The eddies were a welcoming purgatory between rapids, seemingly placed by an act of providence and strategically prepared among the rocks for voyaging creatures like us. If the team could see us, we would wave our paddles with affirmative excitement. If they could not see us, we'd use our whistle signals, which usually could be plainly heard above the shouts of the raging rapids. Mike and Lee would follow. Mike, because of his size, stayed in the stern while Lee shouted commands and crossbow-stroked, picking his canoe through the rocky venue. Then Bill and Denny would follow with Denny in the stern and Bill in the bow together with the important cook kit. After congratulating one another and discussing our successes and shortcomings, we would venture down the river to the next rapids, which usually was not very far. The rapids seemed to come in bunches, and each needed special attention.

We would usually hear the rapids first before seeing them, and the pitch of the sound would give us some idea about what kind of rapids we were running. If the sound was a high-pitched tinkling, we knew it was making a lot of hungry noise but was unable to really feed itself—vocal but not threatening. We should not have any problems running these rapids; they were only cacophonous riffles or baby rapids.

On the other hand, if the sound was a higher-pitched, teenage-sounding staccato like siblings grabbing for a canoe snack, we knew it would have to be monitored, and a route would be probable. But if we heard the rapids barking like an impatient animal and if we heard a grumbling noise like the hungry bowls of a monster, we knew we were in trouble primarily because we knew the monster was hungry for canoes and was beckoning us into its lair, tempting us to try and pass through its clutches. We would then take every precaution and perhaps even search for a portage with all haste.

Once the rapids came into sight, we could also tell what kind of rapids it was by the way it danced. If the water swayed and occasionally kicked its heels up like ballet dancers doing the tour jeté, inviting us to join, then more care would be necessary, but a route would also be probable. If the gyrations of the liquid dancers were jitterbug category, then an occasional bounce on a rock would be inevitable. It appears jitterbugging rocks were placed haphazardly in the waterway just to test our maneuverability skills. Jitterbugging rapids are careless and bump into one another and, in this case, into canoes when they can. They usually do not capsize canoes but delight in ripping rivets from canoes and breaching canoes by tearing holes in them, as we learned when running through Knife Rapids. We often viewed this type of rapids like looking down a descending escalator in a department store. They were probably the most exciting type or rapids for us to run.

If we could hear the rapids roar and grumble but couldn't see it dance, then the nearest exit was pursued primarily because we knew that a tremendous volume of water was descending and disappearing into an unknown cataract, ledge, or falls and into a cauldron of chewing water and boulders awaiting careless canoes. Oftentimes the falls would be completely hidden, and if we did not listen for its warnings, we could've been upon it and consumed before being able to react—a potential catastrophe.

We used the concourse of the river to vary our speed and determine water depth. The river usually will shoot with the greatest velocity down the center of the river whereby the water velocity is usually the least along the edges/shorelines. This is due to the boulders, trees, and snags that inhabit and guard the shores, which slows the water velocity and scours the center of the river. On the bend of the river, or "oxbow," the water will carve the outside edge and form a shallow sandbar on the inside. When the visibility was good and we wanted to make our best time, we maintained a stream-centered, outside-edge attitude. When difficulties were eminent, we would hug the shore and creep among the boulder-guarded shores, shuddering at the threatening shouts of the roaring rapids in the center of the river. Sometimes we would grasp wet trees and roots like cooperative square-dance partners to advance down the rapids. Whenever possible, we would heroically shoot down the rapids.

To maintain safety, we established some definitive rules for running rapids. First, whenever possible, we would survey the rapids from the head of the rapids before trying to run them. Sometimes Steve would just carefully stand in the bow of the canoe, like George Washington crossing the Delaware River, and cast an eye down the rapids to determine whether or not there was safe passage. And other times, we would shore up and walk along the forest or down the portage trail to get a better view of the cascade while the other voyagers dozed or watched with their chins in their palms while in their secured canoes. Steve would often throw a stick into the rapids to see how the rapids affect the buoyant object. I often felt he was just teasing the licking waters. The stick was often consumed among the river's grunts and growls. We always tried to have a good idea of how we could safely outmaneuver the threatening aquatic terrain. If a route could not be found, the arduous task of portaging was employed. This involved carrying the canoes and all the equipment downstream or lining the canoes through the rapids with the ropes at the ends of the canoes. The river already had its quota of victims years ago, and we did not want to become a statistic. Never investigate the mouth of a roaring lion, and never investigate the mouth of a roaring rapids without a planned strategy. Rapids should be respected and reconnoitered before proceeding.

The second rule was to keep the canoe straight down the rapids as much as possible. Getting turned sideways in the rapids can be disastrous and will surely cause the canoe to capsize or be wedged in boulders and destroyed. Even standing waves higher than our heads (that we encountered) could be tamed if the canoe was maintained in an orderly downstream attitude. Even when our canoe was filled by three-foot standing waves, our canoe maintained its buoyancy and control. We simply kept paddling straight down the rapids, half submerged but buoyed up by the air in our packs.

The third rule was to stay with the canoe whenever possible. This was to maintain buoyancy and to protect ourselves, the canoe, and the gear. If a canoe should capsize, then the ejected paddlers should grasp on the *opposite* canoe gunnels at the *upriver* end of the canoe. This will prevent the paddlers from being pinned between the canoe and a boulder. Water hydraulics have awesome power, so they must be treated with careful respect.

The fourth rule is to maintain a *feet first* position when going downstream in the rapids when in the water. If jettisoned from the canoe or if staying with a capsized canoe, it is safest to keep one's feet directed *downstream*. This allows the ejected paddler to see what is coming and to block any boulders that might pin them, with the knees acting as shock absorbers.

Another rule of the rapids is that the sternman should be prepared to jump out while maintaining a grasp of the canoe gunnel to dislodge the canoe from a torpedoing boulder or from dragging in the shoals. This will keep the canoe in a downriver attitude. If the bowman were to jump out first, the front of the canoe would buoy up and pirouette the canoe sideways into an uncontrolled, disastrous position.

Spacing and signaling are important when running rapids. This is important so a canoe in peril can receive help and so canoes do not pile up in the rapids. The lead canoe goes through and glides into an eddy. Raising the paddles aloft signals safe passage and okays the next canoe to follow. Whistles can also be used for signaling. Then the next canoe/s follow/s the protocol until all canoes are accumulated in the safe eddy, prepared to paddle to the next challenge. If the rapids are exceptionally challenging, then the last canoe should portage downstream in advance and await the other canoes that might encounter difficulties. The canoe in front should always be visible to the second canoe, and the canoe behind should be visible to the preceding canoe.

Steve and the author waiting in an eddy

On windy lakes, it is essential to stay close and quarter the waves. If need be, the canoes can be attached side by side for stability with bungee cords or rope.

Finally, the obvious rule, but I will mention it anyway. Personal floatation devices (PFD/life preservers) should always be worn while on moving water. We all had good quality PFDs zipped up and secured, and we wore them consistently. The only time we took them off was on flat water in very warm weather.

With each rapids we conquered, there was a sense of great joy and accomplishment. We saved a great deal of time and work by not portaging and, instead, overcoming our fears. Triumph is not over rapids but over fear. Rapids are not to be treated with contempt but with respect and joy. Maneuvering through the labyrinth of rocks and boulders gave us confidence to the point of being cocky, which can be dangerous. With each rapids we passed, our confidence soared. And the more confident we became the more difficult rapids we could transcend. Running rapids became contagious and something we all looked forward to. There is pride in struggling through threatening rapids of which laity know nothing.

Nevertheless, nature rules! The paddler needs to move to the rhythm of the river and work with her, taking advantage of her mood and the grace she might provide. Follow what she provides because rivers have no mercy; rivers do not forgive.

Bill and Denny joyously completing a rapids run

Mike and Lee completing a rapids run and gliding into an eddy

Rivers are precious, and they may be considered living organisms, not a natural resource. I don't like referring to any river or water area as a resource, like something to be used up. I like to think of rivers as a living organism consisting of a series of systems with organs to support these systems.

Let me explain: An organism is comprised of a number of systems, and a number of organs work together to compose a system. Fish make up a major part of the limnological system. Other systems include the chemical and physical (i.e., temperature, oxygen, geologic, and others). Perhaps rivers should be described akin to the *binomial nomenclature* protocol as exercised by biologists. Water and rivers are precious and should be respected as living organisms. The joy of rivers is not only in the fish they might yield or the rapids they provide, but the real joy is just in knowing their value and studying them.

Chapter 12

Sailing

That's what a ship is, you know—it's not just a keel and a hull and a deck and sails, That's what a ship needs. But what a ship is, really is, is freedom
—Capt. Jack Sparrow

Sailing some of the large lakes proved to be one of the most delightful and rewarding experiences of our voyage—delightful because we could socialize, repair equipment, and dry clothing on the shrouds while under sail, and rewarding because we improvised our canoes into an effective little sailing vessel, which efficiently captured the wind, skipping us across the lakes with ease like a dragonfly depositing eggs. This feeling of improvisational accomplishment was rewarding, and we took pride in our ship.

Sailing was safe and saved time. Many of the lakes we crossed were large flashing freshwater inland seas, and it was safer to sail them together than to try and "grunt" across the otherwise ardent obstacle singularly. We usually had to cross the intimidating sea from the Hayes to the lake inlet and then cross to its outlet at the distal end. This would mean that we would be exposed to the elements and at nature's mercy, so we attempted to traverse the waters as quickly and safely as possible. It was safer to sail because the lashed-together rafted canoes were more stable than paddling loaded canoes individually. What little water was taken in over the spray skirts and equipment was easily bailed out, and with the stability of the three canoes side by side, the chance of overturning or swamping was greatly reduced. We could relax and unwind more safely.

Sailing also saved energy and provided an opportunity for our hands to heal and arms to rest. Paddling across a large lake was not as enjoyable as running challenging rapids, but paddling across a large lake is just a lot of worrisome toil. Besides, our hands would become raw from wrestling and cranking on the paddles in the rapids where we dodged constellations of rocks in the fast-sliding liquid of seemingly endless space, so we'd need to rest our hands. We knew there would be more rapids to run between each set of lakes, and that is where we would need all of our energy and skills, not in paddling placid waters. So sailing the length of the lakes was implemented to save time, energy, and flesh to prepare for the imminent rapids.

Constructing the sailboat was an enjoyable Huckleberry Finn exercise. Once the inlet of a lake was completed and we could see the vast lake expanse, we would check the wind. If the wind was desirable, we would quickly construct the miracle vessel. We would gently shore the canoes side by side and jump into action, each crew member with their assigned duty. Lee would grab the folding saw and down four birches about four inches in diameter and twelve to fifteen feet high. Straight trees were desirous because they would be easier to rig. I lopped off the limbs with my survival knife. We did not like sacrificing living foliage, but dead birches proved to be too fragile; they broke easily and were rejected. Using dead trees might adversely affect our safety, so we pretended we were visiting beavers and released the poles at the end of the lake as a gift to native beavers.

Now the real construction began. We would lay two of the poles across the fore and aft thwarts and securely attach them with wrapped bungee cords that we wisely brought. The bow of the craft was made slightly narrower than the stern, providing a fantail effect so that water would not build up between the canoes. This would also make the canoe track better and thus, make it more navigable. We also left about six inches between each canoe so they would not rub against one another as we crossed bumpy waves. This also provided a wider base, thus more stability. A conventional sailboat's beam is 1/3 wide as the length of the vessel, which our little boat exceeded. The middle canoe would act as the center of directional activity like a nacelle of a P-38 Lightning fighter.

Building the sailboat

Now the mast was to be erected. The mast was fashioned from two more of the birch poles with the bases positioned and secured behind the two front seats of the outside canoes. The upper ends, which were about ten feet, were crossed and tied together. The crossed spires were slowly and carefully hauled upright, aided by a strong nylon line (rope). This line was tied fast to the bow and stern of the middle canoe tightly. Just before hoisting the mast, two flags were attached to the masts and aft line. A small ribbon flag was attached to the highest point on the mast to act as a telltale wind indicator. This would aid in tacking the boat through side winds. Our banner was also attached to the aft rope (line) to also indicate the wind direction and to give us some identity. I proudly took along a Rochester flag as our banner because it was our home city's 105th anniversary. Interestingly, the Cree children were curious as to what country we were from when we stopped in Oxford House.

With the raising of the masts and the banner, the canoes really started to look like a serious sailboat.

Now the sail needed to be improvised. The sail was a large ten-by-twelve-foot nylon sheet that I normally used as a cooking fly. It proved to be the ideal size for our craft, and we could also continue to use it as a cooking fly when we dismantled the boat and camped. It would be a square rig rather than a triangle sailing sheet. An upper and lower boom was fashioned from two more ten-foot birch poles that we gleaned from the forest. The sail was attached to the two booms with light nylon cords through the grommets in the corners of the sheet/fly. The middle of the lower boom was attached to the middle canoe's bow, and the upper boom was attached to a nylon rope that ran over the crossed lashings at the top of the masts. This enabled us to raise and lower the sail easily. Cords with snaps on them, which I fashioned beforehand, were snapped on each corner of the booms and were gathered into the middle of the center canoe. They were used to position the sail into the correct angle to the wind for maximum efficiency and power.

Grasping the wind and sailing

Developing the sailboat was a learning experience. At first, we just lofted the loose sheet without outstretched booms, which proved very ineffective. So we added an upper boom, which proved better, but it was still not efficient. Then we added the lower boom, which produced ample power with even a slight breeze. We joked that we passed through several centuries of sailing evolution within a few hours. It was amazing how much power the boat attained from even a gentle breeze.

Our first rudimentary sailboat without booms

Now the ship could be loaded. The packs were snugly laid in the bottom of the canoe to conform to the shape of the hull, and the safety lines were threaded through the shoulder straps to ensure they would stay with the boat if a turnover occurred. Anything that we thought might be needed without getting into the packs was kept at the top and accessible. This might include rain gear, binoculars, a map, a compass, lunch, cups, sunglasses, and sun lotion. Then the canoe packs were covered with the spray skirts.

Now we were ready to board and set sail. We had to reorganize our seating positions to make room for the masts, lashings/lines, and sail sheet and to maintain control of the boat. The navigator/s usually sat in the bow of the boat with a map and compass at the ready. The rudder men (usually two) would sit in the stern, using their paddles as rudders. The sail man sat midship in the middle canoe, grasping the lines from the ends of the booms to control the action of the sail and take advantage of the wind. The navigators were usually Steve, who sat on the port (left) side, and Lee, who sat on the starboard (right) side. They kept the maps displayed in front of them with their compasses atop to maintain the desirous bearing and watched for landmarks and obstacles. The rudder men were Denny, who sat on the port side, Bill, who sat starboard, and Mike, who sat astern in the middle canoe. I served as the sail man and sat midship in the middle canoe and atop the packs and spray skirt, ready to tack the sails.

Lee sipping Kool-Aid while navigating

Steve navigating and checking maps

Now we were ready to shove off and advance toward our goal, the other end of the lake where we would rejoin the Hayes River. The sailing process was fun but required cooperation and skill. All "hands" would have to work together to attain maximum efficiency of our boat and to maintain direction and safety. First, we would shove off, careful to not breach a slicing gash into the canoes on any projecting rocks. Next, we would face the sailboat into the direction we intended to go. Then we'd check the flags on our mast and the lines relative to the wind direction and velocity. If desirable, Mike would hoist the sail, and I would swing the sail around and try to capture as much of the free energy as possible. If everything went according to plan, the sail would pop full and come to life, and the sailboat would obediently snap into joyful power. Suddenly the rigging would shudder, and the sail would become stiff as iron. And then we could sense the good feeling of moving freely and hear the gurgling water under the bow. She sailed with confidence and grace and straight downwind with authority. Looking back, we could see the wake of the powerful sailboat. Sometimes the wake behind us was substantial, and someone would offer waterskiing lessons. But there were no takers.

Mike could steer well by bracing against his paddle rudder in his canoe stern, but sometimes Denny, Bill, or both of them would help when the wind was violent or when we were tacking at an extreme angle. Tacking is traversing at an angle to the side wind, and we discovered it was difficult to tack with our boat because we lacked a sailboat type of keel. But with our windward sternman, Mike, manning the rudder and Lee and Bill paddling lightly, we could tack to a certain degree well. We tried improvising a keel from extra paddles we had, but we had little success in the threshing water between the canoes. Considering all the obstacles, steering was a major discipline, which Mike handled well.

Mike manning the rudder while Bill trolls for fish

Controlling the sail was another matter that I personally attended to. I held the gathered control cords that determined the sail's angle, but I soon learned it was a boring occupation. I learned that I could lay down on top of the packs and read while holding the lines. Then I discovered I could control the sail with my bare foot in the looped ropes. Eventually, I learned to nap this way with my foot being the autopilot. What joy to sail!

Navigation was critical. Before shoving off, we would carefully determine the bearing from the map to the next Hayes's outlet and try to maintain that bearing. Sometimes an island was in line with the outlet, which made for a convenient stopover and a chance to reconfigure the bearing and possibly have lunch. The lakes were large and often contained a myriad of false bays, which led to no place. Getting lost in one of those bays would mean hours of wasted time and toil, so we stayed away from these aquatic traps.

Some of the lakes contained a maze of small islands, hindering the navigation task by presenting obstacles to the calculated bearing. Only the large islands were designated on the maps, so we had to guess several times whether an island was large enough to warrant sailing. The island often proved to be our allies. When we would paddle against the wind, we would streak from one island to the next like chessboard pieces for sanctuary and solace from the tormenting wind and invading waves. This was especially true on Oxford Lake, where we paddled against the wind and whitecaps all day, only to get drenched at our destination—Oxford House.

On the river, Steve expertly handled the navigation chores about 90 percent of the time. He constantly would be twisting his head right, left, and around, looking for landmarks, then he'd glance down at the map cradled in his lap and make mental note of our position. Usually, he could determine our position by landmarks along the river. This was important in determining time, distance, and daily goals.

On Knee Lake, when we became disorientated, Steve used my sighting compass, which was most accurate. He looked through the compass like a well-trained marksman, marking a spot on the horizon to guide us to the reincarnated Hayes River outlet and more rapids.

When I would navigate, I would lay my compass on my pack between my legs, and as I reined in the sail lines, I would command Mike to correct the rudder. This process was necessary because some lakes were so large that no major landmasses were visible. We always double-checked our bearings with other paddlers aboard to ensure accuracy. I tried to always know where we were on the map and note the bearings in my mind. I still remember the fifty-two degrees when we crossed Oxford Lake after all these years.

While sailing on the proper course, we could relax and attend tasks, like repairing equipment, drying gear, dozing, and chatting, even singing together. Running rapids was especially hard on equipment, so we continually monitored and repaired equipment during any latent time while sailing. The sun usually graciously warmed us while sailing, which made the repairing task enjoyable. On one crossing I dismantled my navigational compass and binoculars to dry them out by laying all the parts in succession on the spray skirt atop the packs in front of me. Like much of the equipment, they were full of water. After drying in the sun, I reassembled the parts, taking care not to lose any of the small screws, back into functioning pieces of equipment.

The compass was an important and cherished piece of equipment. It was an old WWII British commando model that I procured at a gun show and really liked because it was durable and provided several functions. The needle and magnet were inside the hinged *Bakelite* case which also had a mirror inside the lid for viewing the compass face and a slot for viewing distant objects to use as bearing sites. The mirror could also be used for signaling in case of an emergency. The needle was secured and prevented from bouncing around by an ingenious cantilever device when the lid was closed. A ring was built into the base for a lanyard to prevent loss. The glass face of the compass was held over the compass needle with a small rim, rubber gasket, which apparently did not totally seal anymore. It was held together with four small screws. I kept the device in my left hip pocket and the lanyard looped to my belt. I did not wear it around my neck because it was heavier and larger than most compasses.

Another valued piece of equipment was the small binoculars that I carried with a lanyard around my neck. Donna purchased the binoculars for my birthday for mountaineering, but I found they were especially useful for finding portages and river outlets while canoeing. It too, filled with water and had to be maintained, but a faint mineral line formed on the lenses, which remains to this day.

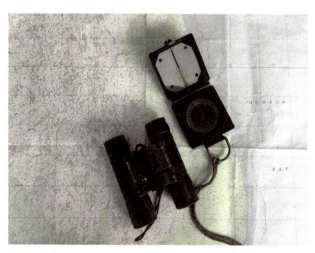

Essential map, compass, and binoculars for navigation

Lee had quite a time with his camera. He initially placed it in the chest pocket of his rain poncho while it was raining on the second day of our trip. To his horror, the camera was filled with water when he took it out to take a picture. The camera would not function after several attempts, so Lee finally took the film out, shook out all the water that he could, held it next to the fire in the evening, and set it out in the sun in his canoe. He continued the process until it was resurrected a couple of days later, and he resumed taking pictures.

Other members of the paddling crew did other things like repairing fishing gear and sharpening knifes. While sailing, there was always food to prepare and songs to sing.

It appears we were always drying clothes. After the tents were erected, the sleeping mattresses inflated, and the sleeping bags unfurled, clothes were hung up on the line we strung between trees or on boulders or on top of bushes.

We would also dry clothes while sailing with the assistance of the wind and radiant energy. Wet clothing, either from being washed or from running rapids, was draped over everything in the ship. The lines which made up the rigging was a favorite hanging place, and Bill especially liked to hang his trousers on the stern mast support line. That meant that the cuffs extended just down to my eye level as I attempted to watch the flag/telltales and control the sail. I had to crank my head around to see around the togs—an awkward method to navigate by. I am sure we looked like a floating New York City tenant house at times. We never seemed to get enough sleep. We would try to sneak a nap whenever we sailed, stopped for lunch, stopped to scout the rapids, or waited out a storm.

When we sailed, we would take turns snoozing if nothing had to be attended. We were sometimes hunched over but were usually lying back or over the packs and spray skirts. It was always refreshing to doze off to the rocking motion of the maternal sailboat and to wake up to the sound of chuckling water under the sailboat.

Steve usually lay straight back in one of the bow seats and cover his face with his hat. Once, we lost our bearing for a couple of hours due to our dozing navigator, for which he jokingly suffered. Mike would lay back over the stern cowl, dressed in his new *polypropylene* outerwear, and stretch his long legs across the gunwales, holding our course with his paddle while he dozed. It was an amazing feat of sailing! Lee would strip down to his shorts and plaster his body with suntan lotion, then he'd don his sunglasses and lie back on the stern cowl, movie-star style.

Bill usually stripped off all his clothes except for his undershorts and bathed in suntan lotion. We humorously considered him the tourist of the group with his bright-green Sherlock Holmes hat and Fruit of the Loom shorts. His shorts were always amazingly blazing white. He, too, often dozed over the cowling with his beloved spinning rod cradled in his arms like a newborn baby. The line would trail with an anxious lure seeking an unwary northern or walleye. He was awakened several times by a snake-faced northern. We took delight in the frantic antics of the Fruit of the Loom fisherman trying to board the snapping miniature gator.

Denny, who was quiet by nature, was the subtlest dozer of all. He simply stripped down to his swimming shorts and lay back in the stern. Or, and this was a most interesting technique, he cleaned the bottom of the canoe where he sat and curled up in the fetal position in the bottom. He was not visible, and the first time I glanced back, I thought we had lost him overboard while he slept.

As for me, I usually took off just enough clothing to be comfortable. I was concerned about getting a sunburn, so I took special precautions by keeping light clothes on. I usually controlled the sail with my foot as I leaned back with my wide-brimmed hat over my eyes to snooze. Sometimes I tied the lines to a thwart and really stretched out for a grand snooze.

Socializing was probably the most enjoyable benefit of sailing in the relaxed atmosphere. We did not confer often while running rapids, and when we did speak, it was with a serious sense of urgency. Our dialogue while gliding on the silent water was always interesting. We talked about a variety of things, sometimes about the last rains or the weather or how we might improve the sailboat efficiency, but usually, the conversations were totally unrelated to our voyage. Perhaps it was an escape mechanism. Nevertheless, socializing was enlightening. We talked about our past because we didn't know each other well. Then we talked about our future, after the trip. And surprisingly, we talked a great deal about music, especially when somebody started to whistle, hum, or sing an old tune. This would usually stimulate a spontaneous form of "name that tune." We would try to guess when the tune was popular, who sang it, or what movie it was featured in. Denny and I excelled at songs from the '50s, and we both had to be restrained from dancing on the packs in the tiny sailboat. Bill liked Linda Ronstadt, whoever that was. Our music preference stratified us into different age groups—an interesting phenomenon.

During one of our sailing escapades, we decided to name our trusty sailboat. After all, it was now a sailing craft of renown. Denny suggested the best name. He decided *Kon-Tiki* was appropriate. The *Kon-Tiki* was a forty-six-foot raft that Thor Heyerdahl and several men made and sailed on for 101 days using primitive methods, travelling from Peru to the Polynesian islands in 1947. The three hundred or so miles we sailed was far less the five thousand miles the original *Kon-Tiki* sailed, but we were proud of our achievement and sailing prowess. We sailed before the mast/s of our *Kon-Tiki* with joyful cooperation, unlike the motley crew of Jack London's *Ghost*. Time was often lost while sailing, and sometimes we would be chatting when a sudden silence would overcome us. A quick glance around would reveal that I had been abandoned by my shipmates for dreamland. Then, just as suddenly, someone would awake and begin chatting again, sometimes on the same subject, almost as if the welcome nap was a comma in the string of ideas being conveyed.

When we would stop for lunch, usually on an island or outcropping, it would take Bill a few minutes to slice the cheese, the sausage, and bannock and mix the Kool-Aid. The others, including myself, would kick off our shoes, lie back on an exposed rocky surface, cover our eyes with our hats, and doze. Just a minute or two was refreshing and gave us new energy. The call to food would bring us back to reality and thoughts of things to be done.

The author napping after lunch on a windy point

Bill preparing lunch of bannock, salami, and cheese at one of the portages

Steve and I often caught a member or two of the group dozing while we were scouting rapids, especially if we left our canoe and walked some distance down a portage to view potential problems and the bottom of the rapids. We would return to find several bodies humped over or laid back in eternal bliss. We giggled but often felt guilty for awaking them.

The gentle rocking of the sailboat and the gracious sun dancing on our faces felt so good that we often had to look around to see if we were still moving or dreaming of moving. On the lower end of

Knee Lake, I began to dread the thoughts of running rapids again, for sailing seemed to defy time—because in ecstasy, there is no measure of time.

On several occasions, we were forced to sit in the canoes to wait out heavy rain and storms. We would put on our rain gear with hoods draped over our heads and sit in the canoes with our heads bowed as if we were meditating monks prayerfully dozing. If there was really no place to go, we stayed in our primary shelter, our raingear, and dozed. Only when the rhythm of the raindrops ceased did we resume our task of paddling.

When we stopped to camp, we each assumed our duties, and work was accomplished with silent efficiency. By nightfall, we were usually too tired to converse because we longed to crawl into our sleeping bags. Entertainment was the last item on our minds. Sleep beckoned us.

Building the Sailing Boat

Care must be taken in handling the handsaw, hatchet, and knife because the wilderness is a terrible place to have an accident. Gloves and safety glasses are recommended. About 20 minutes are required to construct the sailboat, so at the lake's approach the crew needs to determine if the effort for building the sailboat will save time and effort or if it would be expedient to simply paddle the lake. Once it is determined to build the sailboat, construction can begin. The task is easier and quicker by dividing the labor among the crew. That is, a couple members construct the cross mast, a couple building the booms and spread the sail (sheet), and a couple cutting and placing the cross beams.

1. First find a calm place to line the canoes side-by-side close to shore in shallow water. Be sure to keep all canoes tethered so they do not drift away.
2. Cut two sturdy birch saplings long enough to stretch across all three canoes with a few inches in between so the canoes do not rub. Tightly bungee the three canoes to the fore and aft thwarts. Try to leave a little more space between the

canoes' aft so water does not "pile-up" between the canoes. See figure 1.

3. Now for the masts. Cut two more birch saplings about 15-17 feet long and cross them about 18" from the top and tie them firmly together. Firmly tie about a 20' line halfway around the "X". This line will act as the forestay and backstay lines when the mast is lifted. Place the ends of the masts in the bottom of the two outside canoes behind the bow seats and re-bungee them to the thwart and crossbeam. Carefully have one crewmember hold the masts upright and another crewmember secure the forestay to a convenient strong place at the bow of the middle canoe and the backstay to a strong convenient place at the stern of the middle canoe to keep the masts firmly upright. Keep both lines tight. See figure 2 and 3.

4. Now direct your attention to the sail (sheet). Cut two more birch saplings (booms) slightly longer than the width of the sail. They may be lighter in weight, but still need to be sturdy. Stretch the sail between the booms and tie the end grommets to the booms with the heavier one acting as the lower boom. Tie a line securely at the middle of the upper boom and toss the line over the "X". This will act as the lifting shroud (line) to elevate the sail. Tie the lower boom at the center to the middle canoe thwart. Tie lines to all four ends of the booms to act as "tacking" line. See figure 2 and 3.

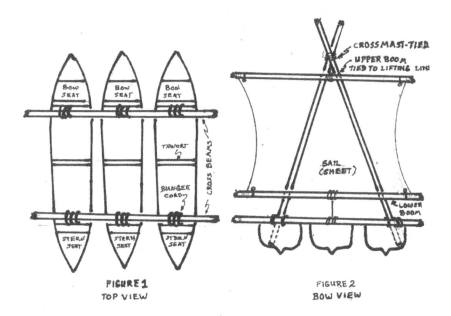

FIGURE 1
TOP VIEW

FIGURE 2
BOW VIEW

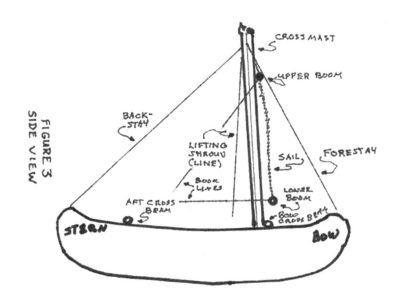

FIGURE 3
SIDE VIEW

Care now needs to be taken because you now have a "live" sailboat! Practice lofting the sail in calm water and soft wind. Distribute the load of the canoes and crew to better control the sailboat. Paddle out into the wind before hoisting the sail. Hoist the sail and fasten the lifting shroud (sail hoisting line) securely to the middle canoe thwart. The boat will respond, and you will be sailing.

It is easy to stow the sailboat intact while stopping at an island to camp or rest. Simply pull into the lee side of island and untie the lower boom and rollup the sail on the lower boom and secure to the cross mast. Be sure to secure the sailboat so it will not drift away or rub on rocks. Upon reaching the river outlet, the sailboat should be dismantled, and saplings left for the beavers.

NOTE: In some areas harvesting saplings might be illegal or ill advised. The cross beams, masts, and booms could be designed and made in advance from heavy PVC or aluminum tubing. They then could be stowed in separate canoes while running rapids.

Chapter 13

The Hudson Bay Sojourn

Wherever you go becomes a part of you somehow
—Anita Desai

We only spent three days at York Factory, but the visit made a lasting impression on us. And it seemed like we spent more time there than we realized. I think it was because we packed so much into our being at this historical, tranquil place where we could be alone to quietly meditate, discover, and reflect. It was a place where we could search for artifacts and reason who was there, what happened to them, and what their circumstances were. It was also a place to be guided by Doug through the past with his waving cane and hear about how it really was. I felt at peace at the bay, especially at York Factory, but I really cannot tell why I felt at peace and tranquil. I get this melancholic feeling whenever I visit important historical places where important things happened; it's like I am revisiting the occurrence in a time warp.

York Factory was *really* a factory at one time. It was a bustling little metropolis comprised of about fifty buildings and a multitude of busy French, English, and Cree workers. It was an important port on Hudson Bay where the two big rivers, the Hayes and Gods, emptied their waters.

The factory was the most important coastal port for the Hudson Bay Company for many years. It received trade goods from Europe for distribution to isolated posts inland. Valuable furs that were received from the posts were shipped to York Factory via canoes or

York boats—small sailing vessels where hides were sized, bailed, and shipped to England, many to be made into beaver hats that were vogue and desirous at the time for men.

The dominant structure was the warehouse that was built in the 1830s, where all the hide processing occurred. The design of the structure was quite unique because it was large and built by shipbuilders who constructed the walls and roof like an inverted ship's hull. The walls were built independently from the floor so the shifting permafrost would not cause structural damage to the entire structure. The leveling of the building was maintained by a series of strategically located hammered wedges. Because of this unique design, the building has lasted many years and is the oldest building in Canada still standing on permafrost.

The design of the warehouse was also unique because it was four buildings placed together with a courtyard in the center, almost like a little fort. It was stately with three floor levels and with ample protection in the courtyard for the women and children in case of an attack and protection from marauding polar bears. Doug explained that there was only one recorded instance when the women and children were gathered there, however. The courtyard was crossed with boardwalks, so it was not necessary to pass around the entire building outside to access the other side of the building.

According to an informative brochure provided by the Manitoba Minister of the Environment, in addition to the warehouse and York boat building, there was a doctor's house, an Anglican church, a library, a cooperage, a blacksmith's shop, a bakehouse, a middlemen's dwelling, a net house, a powder magazine, and a graveyard. Just south of the fort was a Cree village. The only buildings left were the warehouse and one of the old York boat assembly buildings that had been converted into a cabin for Doug. I am not sure what the building we were staying in was. From the lookout tower on top of the warehouse, I could see the strategic importance of the fort. It was situated on a marshy peninsula bordered by the Hayes estuary. For this reason, it held the key to the fur riches of the western interior. France and England battled each other on several occasions to dominate the fur trade.

Prince Rupert, the cousin of Charles II of England, established the Hudson Bay Company in 1670 to monitor lands around the bay and develop its prosperous fur trade. The Hudson Bay Company named the collection and shipping port Fort York in honor of James, the duke of York (who later became King James II) and second governor of the company. The French captured the original fort in 1694, then the British recaptured it in 1696. And then the French captured it again. Finally, the Utrecht Treaty gave the facility complete authority over the entire Hudson Bay region to England, and in September 1714, the French surrendered the fort. In 1788, Chief Factor Joseph Colen ordered the fort to be rebuilt a short distance up the Hayes River to its present location to escape the yearly floods.

It was at this location that the York boats were manufactured, and the name York Factory evolved. But York Factory's days were numbered. When the southerly route through the Red River Valley to St. Paul was discovered, the York Factory was only used for coastal trade because the northerly route was more difficult. The beaver fur trade was decimated when the silk hat replaced the beaver hat as the choice for men in Europe. Most of the trading had subsided by 1874, but the post remained open until 1957—when the doors were finally locked. In 1968, the Hudson Bay Company presented the site to the government of Canada.

Having sailed and canoed much of the waterway between Oxford House and York Factory, I was intrigued by the York boats that were manufactured at the site and maneuvered this route and more.

The York boats were used from 1850 until the 1920s to transport trade goods to Oxford House, Norway House, and other forts along the way. They were forty-two feet long with a thirty-foot keel and a nine-foot beam. Although they were built well, they usually did not last more than three years. I would imagine all the rocks we passed along the way had something to do with the boat mortality rate. Once their usefulness was terminated, the boats were burned, and the nails and other hardware were gathered in the ashes to be reused in new boats. Anything metal was valuable and recycled whenever possible. Each boat carried nine thousand pounds of cargo divided into ninety-pound individual packs, one for each of the nine crewmen to carry, if needed.

York boat once used on the Hayes and Lakes

The crew must have been made up of hardy men because they had to often row the laden vessel down- and upstream and carry all the goods and the York boat over all the portages. As Doug remarked, "That was work." His implication was that we were only having fun running the river downstream. The York boats, however, were equipped, like our *Kon-Tiki*, with sails to catch a breeze. And some of the portages were fitted with winch-operated trams, but the toil, nevertheless, must have been awesome. I cannot help but admire these men.

Most of the trip-men were Métis and Scottish mixed bloods who did all the backbreaking work. They were generally small in stature because a small man could carry more per their body weight than a heavier man and, because they were lighter, could carry more material in the canoe. They usually trotted with the packs on their backs (sometimes double-packing) to save time and elude the insects, but the backbreaking work left many of them crippled and with hernias before they reached middle age. They were a fun-loving group, I understand, because some of the material I read indicated that other members of the fort could not sleep for days when the trip-men returned. It appears they liked to party a great deal when they got back to the fort. It is no wonder; it's because they would be gone for months at a time with a pent-up need for levity.

Chapter 14

Artifacts

The love of old things is a way of respecting time
—Wu Ming-Yi

At low tide, we ventured out to the shore to search for artifacts. As directed by Doug, we carried our whistles, and I carried our .270 caliber rifle to scare away any bears that we might encounter. According to Doug, they do not like high-pitched or loud sounds. By the same token, we did not like low-pitched growls. Polar bears reportedly fake fear of people, which was a concern for us.

Doug informed us that we could salvage things from the sea at low tide. Canada has an artifact law that prohibits the removal of artifacts from landmasses, so we could not glean artifacts from shore or on land. Even with the restrictions, we found a myriad of artifacts in the water. Steve found a small cannonball and a beautiful brass swivel from a trade rifle. Denny picked up a giant clevis, which was quite heavy, and a unique 16-gauge brass reloader. Lee was the best prospector. He found several old keys and an old trade axe head. I found a rusty old ceremonial knife blade and a nice Hudson Bay Company lead seal, the type they used on fresh shipments. Mike did not search much; he spent most of his time toiling over the stove or chatting with Doug. He was good at that. Bill wandered up the north shoreline and did not mention his findings. We all found a multitude of nails and spikes that were used in constructing the York boats. Boatbuilders would burn the old boats and collect the resulting nails to construct new boats, so there were many of those nails still lying on the shore. Doug explained that the flattened nails were the oldest and most valuable, so we kept several. We also uncovered a pair of old anchors and an ancient rudder. But since they were too heavy to salvage and take home, we placed them on the shore to be taken to the warehouse later for display. I also picked up a large quantity of valuable black flint for knapping into flints for my flintlocks back home. It was a treasured find for me. There was a large amount of flint scattered about the shoreline, and I imagine the Cree used the same materials for their trade rifles and for starting fires. Several of us found .72 caliber musket balls that were used in the trade rifles and a .45 caliber shot that was used for harvesting large numbers of geese. Several geese could be killed with one shot. It did not sound sporting but may have been a necessity. I was joyfully surprised when Steve gave me his rifle swivel and Deny gave me the reloader. They knew I admired their finds.

Some of the eclectic artifacts we gathered in low tide mud

Chapter 15

The Cemetery

The cemetery is full of indispensable people
—Winston Churchill

One afternoon, when there was little to do except wait for the boats to arrive, I decided to stroll alone across the stream via a wiggly footbridge to the cemetery, which Doug had improvised. The day was warm, still, and silent. The first thing I noticed was the foundation of the old church, which I had seen pictures of in the storehouse. The fieldstone-and-mortar walls were intact, thick, and about three feet high. The rest, according to Doug earlier, was made of rough sawed wood and sheet metal. The structure was built to last, and it did. But it was now reclaimed by nature.

    I stood in what was once the doorway opening, which overlooked the bay, and fantasized being a voyageur dressed in the typical white shirt they usually wore on Sunday mornings, saying, "Good morning," to the priest and others. Suddenly I realized that the congregation was still near, except now they were muted by death and time. So I continued my stroll around the remains of the church, looking at the "planted" congregation. Each silent grave had its own personality. Some had rough, hand-hewn wood head markers with names and dates crudely carved into them, some had bleached and weathered headstones with names and dates barely discernable, some had headstones made of native stone, and some had no markings at all. Most of the graves had some type of fence around them, all individually designed and unique and mostly made of wood. The fences were designed to discourage bears and wolves from digging up the defenseless occupants—a theory that must have worked because most of the fences still stood vigilantly. Some of the graves had several trees now growing out of them. How appropriate that these early settlers should nourish the land that supported them.

Cemetery plots with wooden fences

By looking at the dates, I could discern that many graves were of babies and youngsters shortly after the turn of the eighteenth century. I later learned that a smallpox epidemic wiped out most of the people at York Factory during that period. It must have been a tragic experience for both the dying and survivors.

One grave was quite impressive. It caught my attention from afar, and it was a struggle to squirm my way through the overgrown alder bushes, trees, and fences to inspect. It had a more elaborate headstone made of fine marble with the name and date plainly visible. The grave was strangely void of trees and vegetative growth on the sun-drenched site, almost like it was being maintained. It was surrounded by a shiny white metal fence with "spear tips" at the top. I surmised that the grave belonged to the factor (chief boss) at the York Factory or to some HBC dignitary. Even in death, the Hudson Bay Company maintained status for those that served the company well.

Factor burial site with iron fence

    I cautiously strode my way back toward Doug's challenging footbridge, still studying the headstones, but I stopped short at the edge of the cemetery, turned, and took one last look around, almost as if expecting to see someone, perhaps a voyageur waving goodbye. I did not have a spooky feeling being among all these silent courageous people; it was more of a feeling of honor that gripped me. I felt honored that I could spend the afternoon mingling with them and "worshiping" with them. They must have been a hearty breed of people, and I was proud to have spent some time with them. I felt I was in the presence of history—in time immortal.

One of the many wooden headstones

Chapter 16

Northern Lights

Seeing a bright auroral display may be on your list of 'things to see before I die'! Yep, they are nature's light show par excellence.
—Jean Tate

One evening, we had a special celestial treat while at the bay. We were all chatting in the red cabin when suddenly Steve came running into the cabin with eyes and mouth agape like a child on Christmas morning. He gestured up with his arms spread and gasped. "The northern lights are out!" We all ran for the door. Mike and I wedged together in the doorway. We struggled awhile until we both conceded and gracefully exited.

Going outdoors was like passing into a misty, dreamlike world through a mirror, like Alice going in to Wonderland. Unfolding before us was an enchanting, breathtaking sight with waves of pink, blue, red, and green flashing across the sky. We watched the earth's most amazing free light show until our necks ached. We just stood there in awe, watching the lights dance and listening to the quiet. Nary an insect, fowl, or mammal broke the spell. The pristine event was accompanied by a galaxy of twinkling, uncountable stars. The night was pure and perfect, and we savored it.

After the mesmerization broke, Steve and I scurried back into the cabin to fetch our photo equipment. We set up our cameras on tripods and took many pictures. I even took some time-lapse photos. But pictures could not do justice for the experience.

We remained outdoors until about 2:00 a.m., watching our feature show outdo its predecessor. The *aurora borealis* is an electronic phenomenon that is precipitated by radiation/particles from the sun, or so the scientists claim. But the Cree claimed that God controlled the lights. The latter explanation, I tend to embrace. The only other place I have seen such a spectacle was in Alaska, where we could even hear them humming. Northern lights are always an awesome mysterious experience!

One of the many pictures we took of the amazing light display

Chapter 17

Fishing

Many men go fishing all of their lives without knowing that it is not fish they are after.
—Henry David Thoreau

Ah, the fishing! The fishing really made what could have been a toilsome effort into a trip of piscatorial joy. It was the frosting on our wilderness cake. It brought shouts of joy and laughter when we were tired, wet, and discouraged. An emotional lift. Plus, the taste of the aquatic morsels made our taste buds dance with joy. And the sudden tug of the monsters stimulated exhausted muscles to enthusiastically respond. Fishing, though not our primary objective, proved to be an enlightenment of joy that awoke the little boy in each one of us.

We talked a lot about fishing during our planning sessions, most revolving around what we might expect in terms of fishing success. We knew we would probably catch enough fish to supplement our packed food, but we knew better than to count on fish for meals. I learned through past experiences that fishing success might suddenly cease. If this were the case, it would mean that we might lack nourishment. We did not want to gamble, so fishing was considered a secondary objective. Besides, this was a whitewater canoeing adventure, not a fishing trip. None of us liked the idea of killing a large number of fish; we'd only catch great numbers to be released, if they were biting.

Nevertheless, we all prepared to fish. This meant that we would need to know what species to expect, what equipment we would need to pack, and what techniques to use to ensure success. Space and weight were a primary consideration, so only limited equipment could be packed. In the final analysis, weight dictated equipment to pack.

It seemed as though everyone we talked to told us to take extra heavy equipment. After procuring some of the monster equipment, I sat down one night before the trip, looked at the equipment, and chuckled. I felt it was ridiculous and humorous to haul this monster equipment on a canoe adventure. *Besides,* I thought in between chuckles, *I could take two medium-sized spoons for each giant spoon.* It made more sense to carry more spoons that a large spoon, and my theory proved correct.

I used this medium-weight philosophy in selecting most of my equipment. I decided to take one medium-weight spinning rod and reel, one heavier backup bait-casting rod and reel, leaders, a large number of spoons, an assortment of floating and sinking Rapalas, a jaw gaff, storage tubes and of course, a lightweight fly rod. All proved successful except for the heavy equipment, which I used rarely.

I pondered a great deal before selecting my rod and reel. I was tempted to take my old spinning rig, but I knew the tip was too light. I bought a reasonably priced new rod with a stiffer tip-top. It is important to have a ridged tip-top to properly set the hook and not overplay the fish. The sooner a fish can be released, the greater the chance for its survival. I do not usually take my expensive equipment on excursions because something invariably gets broken or lost. We broke or lost two rods on the trip but had enough backup equipment to share. I was tempted to purchase a new spinning reel, but I finally decided to take my trusty old Mitchel 300, which proved to be a mistake because the reel finally burned out and froze while hauling in a lunker northern toward the end of the trip. I was disappointed until I realized I had used it for seventeen years without a problem. I removed the faithful reel from the rod and admired it in my hand. All the fish I had ever caught with it flashed before my mind's eye. I was tempted to kiss the reel goodbye and toss it into the lake for a proper burial. After some time, I snapped out of my trance and said to myself, "Heck, I'll fix it when I get home," and stuffed it into my Duluth pack.

I nested the rods together into a compartmentalized flannel sheath that Donna made for me. The nested rods were then placed into a yellow (for visibility) plastic tube attached to the thwarts with elastic bands. This was an attempt to prevent breakage. The reels were simply placed in old sweat socks and stuffed among the soft materials in the Duluth pack for protection. Other than the burned-out reel, all my fishing equipment made the trip without being broken. Steve broke an old spinning rod I had loaned him. Mike lost the tip section of his spinning rod the second day but used it anyway. Denny was not a fisherman, so he did not have equipment to bring. But we shared equipment with him. Bill brought the most equipment and used a lot of it. It seemed like he always had his line in the water, and Lee likewise.

I learned that the line we used was critical. We replaced our lines on our reels with fresh twelve-pound test lines and took a spool of lighter six-weight line. The northerns and walleyes relished the spoons and baits cast to them with great gusto, but the brook trout seemed fussier. When Steve caught the first brook trout, I became agitated and immediately cast into the rapids also, but I did not get any kind of strike even after trying a variety of lures, spinners, and spoons. I became disgusted. Suddenly everyone else caught a redbelly except me. I became more disgusted until I realized I had placed a lighter six- or eight-pound line on Steve's reel. I quickly changed the spool on my reel to the lighter line, and my luck suddenly changed; it was not long before I was pulling in one of my favorite trout. For some reason, the trout disliked the action of any lure that was at the end of the heavy line. I felt better after solving the fishing mystery. I was beginning to get a certain amount of fisherman paranoia.

To protect the line, especially when fishing for northerns or walleyes, we added a wire leader between the line's end and the bait. The stainless-steel type of leader in the twenty-five- to thirty-pound class worked well. We had to be especially vigilant of the alligator-like teeth of the large northerns that were caught. For brook trout, however, we simply added a snap swivel. Most of the fish were quickly released to share their adventure with others. We each only kept one walleye or one brook trout for dinner.

One of the decisions we had to make was what artificial baits to take and use. We each took an assortment of lures, so we had the opportunity to field-test a variety of fish catchers.

The medium-sized Eppinger daredevil worked best. The larger ones were less successful and snagged often in the rapids. I used the red-and-white striped ones most often, but the yellow one with red spots and the chartreuse ones worked fine also. I bent the barbs down on several of them with my pliers so I could release them more easily and not overplay them. Some fish would bounce off the barbless hook, but I was going to release them anyway. The seven- or eight-ounce Daredevils were real fish getters, and I was fortunate enough to have packed about a dozen of them.

Rapalas also worked very well, especially the three-inch, two-treble hooked varieties. It did not seem to matter if they were the floating or sinking type; they usually produced fish. But I found the silver-colored or the perch-colored sinking varieties worked best in the rapids. However, Lee had good luck with one of the new deep-running Shad Raps, and Bill had good luck with a large-jointed Rapala until the rapids claimed it. I tried several large Rapalas with three-treble hooks but found them relatively unproductive. The trout just loved the smaller Rapala. The smaller sinking Rapala should be in every wilderness fisherman's arsenal.

I also took some Mepps spinners along to try. I thought they would be good for trout because I often used them successfully at home in Southern Minnesota streams, but I never caught anything on them on our trip. I was quite surprised at their ineffectiveness.

I also took some larger spoons, pork rinds, Lazy Ikes, preserved salmon eggs, Mister Twisters, and hooks and sinkers for using live bait we might forage. The large baits did not work well, and the other terminal gear worked well. So they were just added weight. Even with our weight limit requirements, we had plenty of fish ammo. We never tried any live bait. No matter what is used to catch fish, the most important factor is faith. Having faith in what is used will usually produce action.

Other essential equipment included a pair of needle-nose pliers, fingernail clippers, and a De-Liar all stowed in a small tackle box. The needle-nose pliers were used for extracting hooks and bending down hook barbs. The fingernail clippers were used to trim and clip fishing lines. And the Zebco De-Liar was used to weigh and measure fish of significant size. I was glad I brought the De-Liar even though it was extra weight and of questionable accuracy because we could keep a somewhat accurate record of our catches.

All the fishing equipment was neatly packed in a small lightweight plastic tackle box. The box was only 5" x 11" x 4" and made of flexible plastic so it could be stuffed into the side of my pack. Mike and Lee each purchased a new compartmentalized Plano box, which worked well for them. It was important fishing equipment be accessible for action when fish were sighted or rising or when we were resting.

There was one more essential piece of equipment needed—something to land the snapping northerns! A net was out of the question because a net would be cumbersome to pack and portage. So I made three jaw gaffs with wood handles and a wrist strap. The tip of the gaff did not have a barb but a one-way spring catch that would prevent a fish from escaping. The spring device could be pushed aside, and the fish released unhurt and unhandled. It is a poor idea to handle a fish because the protective slime layer on the fish can be inadvertently removed. A gaff was kept in each canoe for accessibility and always accompanied us anytime we fished. I was quite proud of the way the lip gaffs functioned.

I had one serious fishing goal that I established before we left, and that was to catch one of those four- or five-pound brook trout on my graphite fly rod. This necessitated packing and hauling another rod, but I was more than willing. With this goal in mind, I carefully packed one of my favorite three-weight graphite fly rods in an aluminum tube and my older Pflueger Medalist reels in the tackle box. Then I tried some of my favorite dry patterns, especially some of the Wulf Adams and Irresistibles, and put them in a separate small fly box. I was ready!

I have had a love affair with the brook trout for some time. In 1967, I caught a Field and Stream Distinguished Anglers Award brook trout, and I have never been the same. This fish was caught in Wisconsin and weighed two pounds and eight ounces. I could just fantasize what a four- or five-pounder would feel like on the end of my lightweight fly rod.

I became excited while we were loading the plane at the start of the voyage. I asked Tony, the pilot, "Have the fish been biting?" He responded with a shocking statement, "Not too good. I guess the speckled [what the Canadians call brook trout] are only feeding on the surface. The only way you'll catch any is if you're a fly fisherman." I began to salivate. I did not care if I caught any other fish; all I wanted were those brook trout! Tony's comments haunted me the whole time we wrestled the river. I kept asking myself, "When will we see the brook trout rising and feeding on molting insects?"

To my disappointment, my dream goal was never achieved. We caught large brook trout all right, but by the time we got to where they were, they were not feeding on the surface anymore. I only unpacked my fly rod once, and that was when a surface-feeding northern fooled me.

We had only one basic method of fishing. That was to cast into the boiling water at the base of any rapids or falls. It seemed like the higher the falls and the more violent the water, the better the fishing. Sometimes we would canoe out into the rapids to fish at the other side, but usually, we just fished from shore. Each falls or rapids had a congregation of fish below, waiting to be caught. Seldom were we disappointed. The falls and rapids aerated the water by infusing air and accompanying oxygen, allowing the fish to breathe more easily. Aerated water is also cooler because the water movement enhances evaporation and was thusly cooling, making it more comfortable for fish. Colder water can hold more oxygen than warm water. Rapids or close to the rapids was the place to be.

There were four basic species of fish that we caught, which were northern pike, walleye, brook trout, and whitefish. Each provided outstanding angling action and excellent supplementary food fare except the whitefish that we released because we were not sure of their palatability. The northern pike (*Esox lucius*), or jackfish, as the Canadians call them, made up most of our fishing action. We literally caught and released hundreds of the spoon-hungry varmints, and some of them grow to be a fairly good size. The Manitoba record is 60.5 inches. The largest we caught was Bill's twelve-pounder, or so we estimated.

Northern Pike

Dennis with the first fish he ever caught—a nice norther

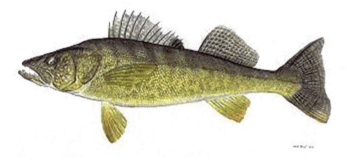

Walleye

The walleye (*Stizostedion vitreum*), or pike, as the Canadians call them, was one of our favorite fish to catch because they were delicious. We caught quite a few of these aquatic delicacies but only kept enough to entertain our palates for the evening meals. The Manitoba record is thirty-nine inches. I believe I caught the largest walleye, and it was in the five- to six-pound class.

The author with nice walleyes from Trout Falls for dinner

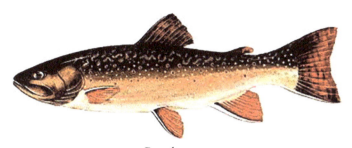

Brook trout

The brook trout (*Salvelinus fontinalis*), or speckled trout, as the Canadians call them, was our most prized fish to catch. It is really a char, not a true trout. It provided the best fighting for its size, so we enjoyed their struggle at the end of the line. The Manitoba record is thirty inches. I think Steve or Denny caught the largest brookie. It was a shade, over four pounds, and a real beauty. They had thick shoulders and bright-crimson flesh.

Steve with a nice brook trout

Whitefish

The whitefish (*Coregonus clupeaformis*) was an exceedingly difficult fish to catch. We would often see them with their tail and dorsal fin sticking out of the water, but they would not bite anything we threw, even flies. The only way we could catch them was by inadvertently snagging them, which we did not want to do. We only snagged two. Bill and I each snagged one each, which we estimated were at four pounds each. We removed the hooks, placed them back into the water, and gave up on the idea of catching any in their delicate lips. After all, who wants whitefish when there are walleyes and brookies to be caught?

Manitoba offers a Master Angler Award for catching and releasing certain sizes of sporting fish. A picture for documentation is required. We had grandiose ideas about participating, but the reality of running whitewater and maintaining our schedule dissolved the idea, until next time anyway.

Every time I see a piece of fishing equipment that faithfully accompanied me on the Hayes River expedition, my thoughts stream back to the majestic river that produced such sporting ecstasy. Surely, if there is freshwater fishing in heaven, it must resemble the base of Trout Falls.

Fishing Rules

NOTE:

If you are planning to go fishing anytime in Canada or any other country, there are several things to consider. First check the current regulations, species bag and size limits, seasons, and special health concerns/warnings. It is easy to do now on computer, which wasn't convenient when we made our odyssey. Be sure to procure your license well in advance and keep it in a waterproof container, like a plastic zip-lock bag. Chances are that it might be difficult to purchase a license once you get to Canada, especially late at night. In several foreign countries that I fished, I had to wait several days before being awarded a license. You probably will not encounter a Mountie or an officer while canoeing/fishing, but you still need to honor all regulations. Fishing is one of the most rewarding and inexpensive activities available.

And don't forget basic fishing etiquette.
- It is best not to overplay your fish and tire them out unnecessarily. Tiring fish makes them easy prey for other animals and can cause them to suffocate.
- Do not grab them through the gills and injure their breathing organs. Only handle them by the jaws. Preferably by not puncturing any tissue.
- Consider using barbless hooks to prevent injury. The barbs can be filed down or bent down by pressing with a pair of pliers. Pressing down the barb leaves a slight bump which will allow you to catch plenty of fish, yet easy to release them by simply grabbing the hook with the pliers and pushing back.
- Don't yank on a hook deep in the fish's throat. Instead, cut the line close to the hook and release the fish unharmed. The hook (never use stainless) will rust and disintegrate within a few days. Best to use circle hooks or artificial baits that usually catch close to the mouth.
- Try not to handle fish by grabbing their body. This removes their protective slime layer. Try to keep the fish in the water to remove the hook and release them as quickly as possible.
- Don't forget to *limit your kill and not kill your limit!* Only keep what you might eat and take quick pictures while the fish is out of the water. Fish are beautiful creatures and too precious to kill irresponsibly.

Chapter 18

Doug McLachlan

The best ships are friendships; may they always be.
— Irish Proverb

Every so often, you meet someone who will make a lasting impression. It might be the way they look, their mannerisms, what they say, how they say things, their values, or some significant deed that they performed that you remember. Doug was one of those people—a person who affected me in such a positive way that I will never forget him, especially when York Factory is recalled. His memory sticks to the ribs of my mind.

He was a stocky man but not overweight. He was quite husky with broad shoulders, which were apparently developed through years of diligent physical toil. His hair was a bold black but was being invaded by the grey of wisdom. He had retired recently, but he was apparently in good physical shape, except he limped badly and therefore was always aided by a hand-hewn cane with a knurl at the top that acted as the handle. He was always clean-shaven, even when we made our unexpected arrival. His face was well featured, weathered by time and experience, and his face was always dressed in a gentle smile and twinkling eyes.

He dressed very simply but neatly. He donned a black Caterpillar hat cocked to one side, a yellow slicker-type rain jacket (always unzipped), a neatly ironed white dress shirt (which begged of a necktie), black cotton pants, and high-topped slip-on rubber boots. He did not carry a hunting knife or firearm, and his hip pocket was void of the normally bulky wallet. He also always carried a foliated willow switch, which he continued to circulate around his head to keep the mosquitos and bulldogs at bay. Whenever he left his cabin, he would always carefully snap off a new switch from the bush along the path. It seemed to be the only weapon he carried. He did not look like a typical hermit or nature seeker.

He spoke with a typical Canadian accent with the last part of each sentence an octave higher than the first, sounding like a question to emphasize a point. I also detected a slight touch of Scotch in his accent. He was fun to listen to as he droned on with limitless yarns. The typical Canadian *aye* was often added to sentences to solicit a response.

His mannerisms were magnetic and entertaining; he was almost like a character actor in some low-budget movie. He spoke softly but with authority. I would often find myself leaning forward toward him whenever he told one of his yarns, trying to catch each softly guided word. But each softly spoken word was articulated in a clear but firm voice. He was not loud or vociferous but wanted to make his point clear.

He was empathetic but analytical. He would often talk about his feeling regarding the Crees and animals and the government, but he would always challenge his own views with the rationale of the opposing view, almost as though he was trapped in a philosophical paradox. It was not because he could not make up his mind, but rather, an attempt to be analytical. He tried to separate reality and idealism in the fashion a backwoodsman would—by explaining what happened, how it could have been prevented in the future, and dispatching the solution.

He was gentle but strong-willed. He never bragged about what he had done even when we pressed him to reveal some of his adventures. He had sort of a laid-back attitude but with a crossed-arms-and-chin-up posture. I tried to get him to tell us about his hunting escapades. Most hunters would give gory details of downed stags or attacking bears, but not Doug. He would casually mention what had been harvested and eaten with a pragmatic tone. It was obvious that he did not enjoy killing creatures of the wilds but knew he had to kill to survive at times and only killed out of necessity, not for self-glorifying status. This attitude permeated his daily life. He was not a trophy hunter, and no antlers or bear skulls adorned his cabin.

He listened with interest more than he talked, but he always talked with authority and wisdom. As we chatted, I would note that he occasionally would disagree with one of us on an issue. Instead of arguing, he would carefully listen to the argumentative premises and analyze the resultant conclusion. Then he would respond with a nod and by sitting back in his chair in reluctant acceptance, or he would hunch over with his elbows on the table and shrug his shoulders with a "maybe you're right" body language comment, which was really a silent rejection. Whatever the result, he always respected other opinions and what it intellectually presented, and he expected the same from others.

One vice that he obviously had was that he enjoyed smoking. But even this was done with careful precision. The cigarettes were of some unique brand and were packaged in a single row in a hard cardboard pack. They obviously were not of American origin. Doug only smoked after eating, for I never saw him go through the smoking ritual at any other time. After finishing his meal and carefully stacking his personal tableware, he would reach into his pocket and retrieve his cherished box of cigarettes. He would carefully open the box and admire the small white cylinders like he was trying to select a special one. He then would pluck one from its nest and gingerly tap the end on the lid of the box to firm up the tobacco. Then he would pause like he was expecting a response to his knocking. The cigarette would then be gently pushed into an elongated black cigarette holder. He'd then clench the holder in his teeth in a chic fashion, like a 1930s film star. A match would be struck to life, and the cigarette would ignite and glow with delight for Doug. And Doug would ease back into his chair to enjoy his vice. When he made a dramatic point, he would elevate the holder and glowing cigarette in a pose made famous by FDR. It was entertaining watching him relax and perform at the same time.

Another interesting mannerism was his Hudson Bay vigil. He almost always watched the Canadian flag that he hoisted earlier over the point. Doug would knock punctually at 7:30 a.m. at our cabin door. After being recognized (who else could it be?), he would enter and station himself at the southeast corner of the table and begin chatting while facing the window with his left elbow cocked over the back of his chair and while sipping coffee delivered to him by Mike. Thus, his vigil would begin. If there was any change in the wind that was detected by the flag, he would comment about what effect this would have on the character of the bay. On several occasions, while we were watching for the jet boats, he would note a wind change then jump up and wobble out to the point to check the fog, shaking his cane at the sky as if scolding the weather god. The flag seemed to have a hypnotic spell over him, but we knew better. We knew that he could read nature's signs, which were oblivious to his neophyte visitors.

Doug at breakfast, telling us one of his yarns

Doug's cabin was a treat to visit. It was originally a York boat repair shop that had been converted into a cozy cabin. It had a large glassed porch facing south to capture valuable passive solar heat. Each side of the cabin had two small windows, which were encircled with barbed wire to discourage visiting polar bears. Above the cabin were two hand-hewn pine poles that had a wire lazily draped between to act as a shortwave radio antenna. A shed, which was located about twenty yards away, housed the gasoline engine and electric generator that powered the few appliances and radios that were in the cabin. Of course, there was the outdoor toilet that was conveniently located between Doug's cabin and the one we occupied. He even had conveniently built a boardwalk to the outhouse from the cabins. Everything was clean and painted white, but we could expect that of Doug.

When you walked into his cabin, you first entered the porch, then you had to walk through his bedroom before entering his kitchen/living room. Both cabins had only one door to enter and exit the building—apparently, a practical solution to reduce drafts that accompanied the cold weather and discourage polar bear entry.

Doug was a fussy, immaculate housekeeper. We learned this quickly when we followed him to his cabin to radio home. As he entered his porch, he systematically removed his boots then gestured to us with a square jaw and stout cane to do the same. As we passed through his bedroom, I noticed that his bed was neatly made and clothes categorically hanged up. His kitchenette was spotless. There were no dirty dishes on the counter or in the sink, and the floor was freshly waxed. The windows were squeaky clean, and the sills were freshly painted white, of course. There was a bucket of clean water on the corner of the sink with an aluminum dipper dangling from the rim. The living room area was dimly lit because there were no windows on the north side, but I could still see well enough to note that the quarters were also neat and clean. The walls were covered with wallpaper that had big gaudy flowers, something like a Wisconsin farmhouse from the 1950s. There were a few nicely balanced pictures on one end of the wall and a well-stocked bookshelf on the other side. Doug had a well-diversified library. Most of the books were contemporary, but he also had books about Truman, Eisenhower, and the wilderness. I was a bit ashamed that he knew more about Reagan and former president Carter's foreign policies than I did. He could quote a great deal of poetry with feeling. He had developed quite a liberal education through his many books and cassette tapes without the aid of arm-waving instruction. Doug was a living example that self-motivation is always the best instructor. Finally, the north side of the living room graced a large comfortable-looking couch that was guarded on both sides by two stoic self-supporting gas lanterns. The cabin was an immaculate place to visit, and I would not dare compare it to my house back in Rochester anytime my wife has been gone more than two days.

Doug telling us about his polar bear encounter. Note the shortwave aerial strung out over his porch.

Doug's values were simple and concise. He loved his god, the wilderness, his family, York Factory, and the bay, but he did not have to tell us so. It was obvious in his tone as he said things. He was the patriarch of York Factory and probably should be considered its last factor. He knew every conceivable historic fact about the factory and took pride in sharing his knowledge.

Even though he revered this enchanting place and was the York Factory scholar, he was disappointed that the Canadian government did not recognize his expertise. He had lost his official status at York Factory. Therefore, Chris had been hired as the caretaker, and Doug degraded to volunteer status. We could sense that it bothered Doug and that there was a certain amount of coldness between the two, although, they both respected each other and tried to live within the situation not of their making. Chris stayed at the official abode, and Doug stayed in the white cabin on provincial land. Chris, we could tell, still relied on Doug for leading the tours and to answer questions. A type of reluctant respect was evident.

Doug, although he never really stated so, was a religious man. He always liked to join us in prayer before our meals and had constructed a chapel inside the factory with stained glass windows, pews, and the cross he had rescued from the decaying chapel near the cemetery. He was especially proud, and rightly so, of his chapel. When we visited it, I slid into the uncomfortable pew, gazed at the lead-covered cross, and said a prayer of thanks. "Thanks for guiding me here and meeting Doug."

During the evenings, Doug usually told us about some of his York Factory experiences. Some of them were about his bear encounter, Cree problems, Hudson Bay Company life, and visitations of other paddlers passing through.

One of the most fascinating stories Doug told us was about his polar bear attack. He often encountered the large creatures but could usually chase them away by shouting or by shooting his 12-gauge shotgun into the air. This polar bear encounter was especially tantalizing. An eight-hundred-pound bear came up to his house and pushed on the sides as though sizing up the structure. Finally, the bear came through the storm door to the porch, broke down the main door, and entered the house with a hungry look in his eyes. Doug was ready and dispatched the crazed animal in his living room with his rifle. Upon inspection, Doug discovered that the bear had a broken jaw and was unable to capture seals in the bay. Apparently, he considered Doug for a meal. Doug reported the incident but had to fly into Winnipeg to defend himself before the magistrate, who declared him innocent because he was defending himself.

I still often think of the bay and Doug's stoic vigil. Occasionally, I allow my thoughts to wander to the bay, and I wonder, *How cold is it up there? I wonder what the wind is like. How many paddlers went through this year?* And most of all, I wonder what Doug is doing today. Most often, when I clench my eyelids, I see Doug sitting in painless toil on the weathered bench at the edge of the cliff overlooking the bay with his cupped hand holding up his tired chin, his steel-grey eyes trying to unravel the mysteries of the bay. He'd be sitting there under the scarlet Hudson Bay Company flag snapping in the easterly wind.

When the luxuries and materials of modern civilization engulf me, I often remember Doug's words: "I have everything I need." How great it must be to be that content. The bay was a hypnotic, tranquil place whose real value was in its isolation and bounty. I often miss it.

Chapter 19

Oh, Canada!

I love Canada. It's a wonderful political act of faith that exists atop a breathtakingly beautiful land.
—Yann Martel

The flight over Canada revealed a vast, wild wonderland decked with greenery, accented with azure waterways and lakes, and punctuated with rich buff-colored wetlands! Surely, this is one of the most beautiful and unforgettable sites to behold.

From the Otter; a view of the swath through the wilderness for electrical lines to provide energy for the urban areas.

Although we could write volumes about Canada, I will include only a few facts. According to Wikipedia, Canada is 3.85 million square miles, making it the world's second largest country by total area after Russia, occupying roughly the northern two-fifths of North America. Manitoba alone has seventy-six rivers and sixty-eight lakes to tantalize the adventurer or sportsperson. Canada's lakes, rivers, streams, and wetlands hold 20 percent of the world's freshwater, and this important watershed ecosystem needs to be protected for wildlife and people at all costs. All 167 subwatersheds are threatened by increased pressure of urbanization and agriculture encroaching on freshwater habitats. The demand for energy has increased pollution, and an increase in hydroelectric dams is impeding water flow. I only hope Canada has the wisdom to protect its wonders.

Chapter 20

The Nature of Adventure

*The real voyage of discovery consists not in seeking
new lands, but seeing with new eyes.*
—Marcel Proust

Why subject oneself to strenuous physical challenge, mental dilemma, and possible danger? Why not stay home, safely incarcerated in your living room, satisfyingly fed by the refrigerator and entertained by the TV? The answer lies in the psyche of the individual and in one's value system, goals, and objectives of their life.

The quest for adventure may vary with individuals. Many consider adventure as a way to feed an ego, but egos are rarely satisfied. Others look to adventure challenges as an enlightening experience or an opportunity to learn more about the wonders of nature and how she works. And adventure fulfills that need. Yet others look to adventure as a means to learn more about oneself. One needs to know what their possibilities are. Every fledgling must stretch out their wings and fly…or fall. The recipe for adventure should include physical and mental preparedness, developed skills, and equipment. But adventure is of little consequence without being flavored with reasonable risks! Struggle brings strength, endurance, confidence, courage, and self-esteem—the grit of life. And like life, adventure involves mystery and unfolding drama. Adventure is a way for one to prove oneself to oneself.

The Hudson Bay odyssey was an adventure. Albeit a modest adventure, it was nevertheless an important personal adventure for each one of us. True adventure requires some risk, and herein lies the questions: Why does a person torture oneself? Why does the person subject oneself to offensive elements, ravenous insects, and thundering water? Can adventure and ego fulfilment be so important as to motivate someone to risk life and limb? These are just some of the questions often asked, and they are fair questions that need explanations. I will try to answer these questions with candid openness. To discover, learn, experience, and acquire change are all reasons for adventure. Adventure is not only a euphoric, affective experience but also a cognitive, self-enlightening experience.

Adventure provides the opportunity for us to learn more about ourselves. By reaching out into the unknown, we also reach into ourselves. If we do not stretch, we never know how far we can reach. Our potential is proportionate to our willingness to physically, emotionally, and intellectually reach out. People who never reach out because of personal fears or peer obstruction never experience the beauty and power in themselves. Personally, I wouldn't know much about myself if I did not risk myself physically, emotionally, or intellectually. How better to learn one's values and potential?

For all practical purposes, there is little wilderness left to explore. Most major rivers have been run and mapped. Most continents have been explored and traversed, and most summits have been reached and claimed. Now we need to explore our hearts, minds, and souls—domains many refuse to encounter and consequently never reveal to themselves.

If we do not experience, then how can we empathize? In spite of all the modern visual aids, how can I understand hunger unless I have been hungry? How can I understand thirst unless my throat has begged for quenching? How can I understand cold unless my fingers and toes have cried for warmth? Or how can I understand pain or sorrow unless my body and heart have not been bruised or wounded? No, I don't care to inflict wounds or flagellate myself. It is unnecessary with adventure as the accomplice.

We often hear of the challenge of adventure. Most people probably start with this attitude of subduing the outdoors. The challenge of subduing the loftiest summit or cascading the most vociferous river initially attracts them, but time, experience, and self-enlightenment soon converts them. They change into a higher more introspective species, so to speak. They no longer wish to subdue nature but to absorb it. There is greater pleasure with being in the natural environment and being part of it rather than fighting to subdue nature or natural forces. There is a strange pleasure in being molested by mosquitos and blackflies. With each sadistic pleasure of an insect bite, I am taught humility by being the prey instead of the predator for a change. With every mosquito bite, I am reminded of my fragility. I like to think of myself as a sponge absorbing beautiful and wonderful happenings around me to experience and not to subdue. Discovering the wonders of nature and self are the epidemy of life.

There is, however, the risk of failure that accompanies adventure. But there really is no such thing as failure, only learning. Some will experience failure and quit while others will accept the experience and learn from it, especially if one learns something about oneself. This is what outdoor adventure has taught me. Outdoor adventure is not one major conquest after another. It is success often followed by failure followed by more success—a sequence that can often successfully be found in the odyssey maze we call life—as we develop self-esteem and confidence. This up-and-down experience adds meaning to life. After all, what good is happiness without some sorrow? What good is success without some failure? What good are valleys without some mountains? What good are eddies without rapids? In real learning, there are no failures, only learning experiences. Our "failures" only open doors to new adventure corridors of learning. Failures are only new lessons. Accepting defeat only makes cowards.

But yet there are many forms of adventure. Adventure needs not be just an athletic milieu!

Other adventuresome risks might be in the form of intellectual, emotional, professional, or financial risks, but should be within ethical, moral, or legal parameters. Failure and disappointment need to be willingly accepted.

And adventure should not be confused with a death-wish intoxication where unnecessary risks are taken with an unacceptable challenge to nature—because nature usually wins. Reasonable risks are sensible and wise and include "backup systems" to ensure future adventure challenges. There are other rivers to run and other mountains to climb. Why risk terminating the future?

In terms of existential learning, the outdoor adventure experience can be invaluable. Where else could one learn better of their fragility, their reason for existence, or the presence of God?

I never cease to be amazed as I wander in the environs and take in the intricacies of life and systems. What better way to experience God's creativity? I refuse to believe that all these wonders, including myself, are the result of some cataclysmic comedy of genetic errors. No, the natural systems are too perfect and work too well unless disturbed by people. God also gave us the urge to explore—the result of adventure.

People were not designed to just eat, sleep, reproduce, excrete, and collect. Primitive annelids and other forms of lower fauna do that! There is more to life. Adventure fulfills an innate human need to explore.

We were given a heart, a soul, and a mind to explore and share. Whether we like it or not, each person is on a mission on earth. But each of us must discover what that mission is. After all, the safest place is in the corner of the basement, so why aren't we all there? We all take personal risks for enlightenment and to share our findings. Not all of us take outdoor risks to reach these ends, but risks, nevertheless, are necessary in life. Somebody once said, and I agree, that "we must venture or vegetate, reach or rust, seek or spoil, deploy or decay and strive, not only survive."

So go on an adventure and take some risks. Find out what your potential is and who you are. Find your odyssey!

Afterword

As I sit here at my desk in Homosassa, Florida, looking out my window at the greenery and hearing the many songbirds delightfully chirping, I wonder what is going on up north where it is cold and snowy. Sometimes I really miss it. It has been nearly forty years since the odyssey, and yet what the river taught me still lingers. Nature is always the best teacher.

Writing *A Hayes River Odyssey* was a melancholic journey. With each passing chapter and daily log read, I was drawn back to the river and the bay. After all these years, I can still remember many of the joyful and challenging experiences like they occurred yesterday, each permanently etched on my heart's mind. In a way, the odyssey has never ended.

One thing I learned through my many environmental activities was that beautiful places become unforgettable with wonderful people. Not only on the Hayes but with Myke, our son, canoeing in the jungles of the Congo with the children of Karawa in dugout canoes, climbing the Grand Teton with Bill Jackson, Col. Jim Irwin's climbing team in Turkey, and the many backpacking trips with Donna, my wife, and kids. Each experience was flavored with great people I have grown to love.

But I am saddened by the thought that my outdoor adventures might be over. I have shared the Hayes River odyssey with many groups, and more than five thousand slides I have amassed during the years now lack a projector. I recently sold my Duluth packs at our garage sale without fanfare for a pittance to a young dad who wanted to take his kids to the BWCA. Nobody would buy the cook kit that Mike labored over to make our meals, so I unceremoniously took it and other equipment used on the odyssey to the landfill. I had to remind myself that it was only unemotional equipment. But memories of a dream odyssey fulfilled will last.

The Price of Time

Reflections from tranquil waters
A collection of verses by Minnesotans
By John Kudlas

1981

Reflections from Tranquil Waters
A Collection of Verse by Minnesotans

As I sit in this throne of Naugahyde,
How I dream of the many days gone by,
When money poor, and luxury free,
I was rich with nature's endless bounty,

And all these wonderful things offered free,
Given by God to a lowly man, me.
But I wanted that of machine and man,
So I rejected what was close at hand.

Now I would give a hard-earned million
To ride waters of golden vermillion,
To be baptized with waters of tannic taint,
Which were blessed by stoic conifer saints.

I would even give my last tarnished dime
To push water under me one more time,
To drift silently with the yodeling loon
As if, in air, a helium balloon.

JOHN KUDLAS

But I wouldn't give a nickel of wood
To toil endlessly at what others think I should.
For the end of a hard portage at last
Is the joy in the goal-finding to pass.

Happily I would give my last red cent
To hear the crickets click around my tent,
To lay up the earth's warm still bosom,
Listening to the beat of her wisdom.

But all the worldly money can't return
The wood and time at cozy campfires burned.
The price of time is quickly here and gone
Like the waters the canoe rode upon.

Appendix

(11)

CAMERA EQUIPMENT

____ Camera - 35 mm
____ Lenses/filters
____ Mini tripod
____ Extra film (5-10 rolls)
____ Waterproof bag or box
____ EXTRA CAMERA BATTERIES
____ _____
____ _____
____ _____

GROUP EQUIPMENT

____ Tents/ground cloth
____ Duluth packs
____ Cooking kits
____ Camp stove - LIGHT WEIGHT
____ Siera cup - ONE FOR EACH
____ Folding saw
____ Hatchet/ax
____ Dishtowels
____ Soap
____ Food/menu
____ Sewing kit
____ Cooking fly
____ 1/8" nylon cord (150')
____ Neoprene sealer
____ Large filet knife
____ Cooking rack (grate)
____ CANOE REPAIR KIT - PRE-RIVED
____ SHARPENING STONE SHEET ALUMINUM
____ SHOVEL (FOLDING)
____ CANDLE LAMP - ONE PER TENT

FISHING EQUIPMENT

____ Rod/reel
____ Extra spool of line
____ Spoons - assorted large
____ "Pickled" minnows
____ Pork rind
____ Large hooks
____ Gaff (1/canoe)
____ License
____ Small tackle box
____ Leaders (metal - 12)
____ Needle nosed pliers
____ Plastic worms
____ Sinkers
____ **Mister** twisters
____ RED TUBE
____ REPAIR KIT (EXTRA GUIDES + TIP TOP)
____ FISH SCALE (DE-LIAR)

GROUP ITEMS/CANOE

____ Map
____ Gaff
____ Extra Paddle
____ Life preservers
____ Duct tape
____ Ropes/lines
____ Toilet paper(white)
____ Fish stringer
____ Large plastic sheet (BLACK)
____ First Aid Kit (tape, T-bandages, vaseline blow-up splints, sutures
____ MAPS (IN PLASTIC)

JOHN KUDLAS

PERSONAL ITEMS

CLOTHING

- ~~Pack boots~~ VIET NAM BOOTS
- Camp Boots (light)
- Underwear (short)
- T-Shirts
- Long undershirt
- Pair wool socks
- Pair wool trousers
- Long sleeved wool shirt
- Down (warm coat)
- Widebrim (hat/cap)
- Handkerchief
- Mosquito netting
- Rain jacket
- Rain pants
- Waterproof bags for clothing
- Rubberized gloves
- Wool gloves
- Bandana
- SAFETY PINS

OTHER

- Air Mattress (or pad) AIR MATTRESS PUMP
- Sleeping bag
- Flashlight (SMALL)
- Mosquito lotion (BEST)
- Suntan lotion
- compass
- Notebook and pencil
- Sunglasses
- Duluth pack
- Binoculars (small)
- Hunting/survival knife
- Swiss army knife
- Matches/lighter

TOILETRIES

- Toothbrush
- Soap (ivory)
- Shampoo
- Comb
- Towel (bath)
- Washcloth
- Antacid tablets
- Mirror- unbreakable
- Aspirin tablets
- Small scissors
- Chapstick
- Fingernail clippers

A HAYES RIVER ODYSSEY

IMPORTANT ADDRESSES

CANADIAN CUSTOMS

    Winnipeg Federal Building
    269 Main Street
    Winnipeg, Manitoba R3C 1B3
    (AC204-946-6004)

FIREARMS PERMITS

    Ministry of the Solicitor General
    Firearms Policy Centre
    340 Laurier Avenue West, 12th Floor
    Ottawa, Ontario, Canada K1A 0P8
    (AC613-593-4995)

PROVINCIAL & TERRITORIAL INFORMATION

MANITOBA

    Travel Manitoba
    Department 3020
    Legislative Building
    Winnipeg, Manitoba, Canada R3C 0V8

AUTOMOBILE ASSOCIATION

    Canadian Automobile Association
    1775 Courtwood Crescent
    Ottawa, Ontario, Canada K2C 3J2
    (AC613-226-7631)

AUTOMOBILE INSURANCE

    The Insurance Bureau of Canada
    181 University Avenue
    Toronto, Ontario, Canada M5H 3M7
    (AC416-362-2031)

MAPS

    Mines, Natural Resources and Environment
      Surveys and Mapping Branch
    1007 Century Street
    Winnipeg, Manitoba, Canada R3H 0W4

(over)

JOHN KUDLAS

IMPORTANT CANADIAN ADDRESSES
-2-

POLICE

    Winnipeg Police Department
    6 Donald Street, Room 100
    Winnipeg, Manitoba, Canada R3L OK6
    (AC204-475-3344)

AIR FARE & DROP-OFF CHARGES

    Fly-A-Long Ltd.
    Box 111
    Norway House, Manitoba, Canada ROB 1BO
    (AC204-359-6667)

    Cross Lake Air Service, Inc.
    Box 100
    Wabowden, Manitoba, Canada ROB 1BO
    (AC204-689-2166)

BOAT FLOAT   *Doug MacLachlan* → *WINNIPEG, MANITOBA, CANADA*
    John Hatley   *2280 NESS ST.*
    Big Trophy Outfitters, Box 322
    Gillam, Manitoba, Canada ROB OLO
    (AC204-652-2776)

OTHER NUMBERS

    Department of Natural Resources
    AC204-359-6266

    Clark Wilkie (made trip last year)
    AC204-638-7006

    Hudson Bay Store (Kirk Coats)
    AC204-354-6258

    Horizon Travel (Rail Travel)
    Gillam-Wabowden 2:40a.m.-6:30a.m.
    AC612-474-4152

About the Author

John Kudlas, a retired biology and ecology educator and adventurer, has canoed rivers and lakes in northern Wisconsin, Minnesota, Utah, Florida, Canada, the Congo, and Slovakia. John has received several educational and environmental fellowships and awards and conducted many environmental and outdoor adventure workshops. He has mountaineered in several countries beside America, including Slovakia and Turkey and has published several magazine and newspaper articles and a book about rock climbing skills and related education values.

CPSIA information can be obtained
at www.ICGtesting.com
Printed in the USA
BVHW091300280922
648135BV00003B/70